EDITED BY WESLEY H. BROWN
AND PETER F. PENNER

Christian Perspectives on the
Israeli-Palestinian Conflict

D1637005

EDITED BY WESLEY H. BROWN
AND PETER F. PENNER

Christian Perspectives on the

Israeli-Palestinian Conflict

NEUFELD VERLAG

**Christian Perspectives
on the Israeli-Palestinian Conflict**

Occasional Publications – published in cooperation
with *International Baptist Theological Seminary*
of the *European Baptist Federation* o.p.s. (www.ebf.org)

*IBTS
Nad Habrovkou 3
CZ-16400 Praha 6
Czech Republic
www.ibts.eu, IBTS@ibts.eu*

Cover design: David Neufeld, Schwarzenfeld, Germany
Composition: Markus Neufeld, Bamberg, Germany

© Wesley H. Brown and Peter F. Penner
Publication date: June, 2008
WCIU Press ISBN 978-0-86585-005-7
Library of Congress Control Number: 2008929740
Neufeld Verlag ISBN 978-3-937896-57-1
Best.-Nr. 588 657

www.neufeld-verlag.com

Co-published with:
William Carey International University Press
1539 E. Howard Street
Pasadena, CA 91104
email: wciupress_orders@wciu.edu

Contents

List of Figures

List of Tables

Introduction: European Christian Leaders Face the Challenge of the Israeli-Palestinian Conflict

WESLEY H. BROWN & PETER F. PENNER

Christians interpret the events of the last 60 years in the land of Israel or Palestine in very different ways, with frequent claims to biblical passages for their positions, whether of support or condemnation. Christian Zionists and Palestinian Christian liberation theologians both assert that they interpret Scripture responsibly. Who is right? This book is a collection of articles from an International Baptist Theological Seminary Directors Conference on the topic of "Christian Perspectives on the Israeli-Palestinian Conflict" (Prague, November 13th to 17th 2006). The different articles will endeavour to explore divergent Christian positions presented by both Jewish and Arab spokespersons from the Land and examine their presuppositions and biblical interpretations. Western discussions on the Israel-Palestine issue will be presented in different articles concerning the tension that we find in the West concerning Israel/Palestine and the conflicts of the region. Other articles will also seek to impart information about current efforts toward peace with justice and reconciliation, with a challenge to support grassroot ministries that are built on responsible biblical foundations.

What happens when Israeli and Palestinian spokespersons from Jerusalem tell their dramatic stories to Christian leaders from twenty countries meeting in Prague? Can the leaders find any unanimity of response, despite the pain of the Israeli-Palestinian conflict and the different ways in which Scripture is interpreted and applied to the conflict? Delegates from twenty countries said an unanimous "yes" as they met at IBTS Prague. They were exposed to the painful realities and complexities of divergent Christian Arab and Messianic Jewish positions, and asked how Christians might contribute in some small way to reconciliation and peace with justice. They found a ray of hope in some grassroots efforts within Israel/Palestine to hear and understand one another, and to respond with compassion and help in times of crisis. Delegates pledged their support and prayer for reconciliation and peace initiatives, and challenged the churches to make practical and prayerful contributions in partnership with Christian Arab and Messianic Jewish communities in Israel/Palestine.

Prague Declaration

Meeting at the International Baptist Theological Seminary in Prague, 13-17 November 2006, with Israeli and Palestinian involvement, delegates from twenty countries (Israel/Palestine, Romania, Russia, Kazakhstan, Moldova, Holland, England, Scotland, Northern Ireland, Serbia, Bulgaria, Kyrgyzstan, Ukraine, India, South Africa, South Korea, Czech Republic, Latvia, United States, and Italy) agreed that:

We affirm our faith in Jesus our Messiah and Lord, the inspiration and authority of the Bible in matters of faith and practice, and our love for all peoples.

We acknowledge
— with deep regret the Church's historic role in anti-Semitism. We affirm the right of the State of Israel to exist, free from the threat of annihilation.
— with deep sorrow Christian indifference to and ignorance of Palestinian suffering. We affirm the right of Palestinian self-determination.

We rejoice to learn of the growing number of Jews who are coming to know their Messiah and of the vibrant witness of Christian Arabs in the Middle East.
We pledge our support and prayer for those in Israel/Palestine who engage in reconciliation and peace initiatives, building bridges between people.

We call upon our churches
— to partner with local ministries (Messianic Jewish and Christian Arab) to identify and respond to the needy, starting with the "household of faith".
— to use their influence with governments to promote peace with justice.
— to act with great sensitivity when making public statements about the situation or about other faiths, abstaining from statements that could endanger local believers or discredit their witness.
— to encourage reconciliation efforts in the Middle East.

We pray
— that our churches will inform themselves and support the indigenous outreach/witness of the local Christian Arab and Messianic Jewish communities.
— that all involved parties will seek God's guidance in the pursuit of peace with justice by non-violent means.
— that the Church will exhibit a spirit of love and humility as they view the conflict.
— that the Church will be an agent of healing rather than a source of division in the Israeli-Palestinian conflict.

Prague, Czech Republic, 17 November 2006

A Historical Overview of the Israeli-Palestinian Conflict and Christian Responses

WESLEY H. BROWN

This historical overview of the Israeli-Palestinian conflict comes from someone whose experience and faith have led to a commitment to peace with justice for all people. I lived in Jerusalem for over 11 years as American Baptist representative for the Middle East. At first I lived with an Orthodox Jewish family in West Jerusalem (the Jewish side of the city), and then I lived in East Jerusalem (the Arab side) in an apartment building whose owner was an Arab Christian. That gave me exposure to two contrasting lifestyles and interpretations of history. Later, Cheryl and I served in the Ecumenical Institute for Theological Research at Tantur, on the southside of Jerusalem, overlooking Bethlehem. We worshipped with the Narkiss St. congregation that had both Messianic Jews and Christian Arabs in attendance. For eight years, I wrote a column called "Christian Comment" in the *Jerusalem Post*. Because of that writing responsibility, and during that time, I interviewed and wrote articles about most of the different Christian communities in Israel/Palestine and learned about their very different attitudes toward Israel as a nation and toward its "occupation" (as perceived by Palestinians) of the West Bank and Gaza, or, as many Jews prefer to call the area, "Judea and Samaria". Of course, things have vastly changed since we left Jerusalem, but we have tried to keep informed by many returns to Israel/Palestine to lead seminars. We have renewed friendships, listened to the pains and hopes of both peoples, read and prayed, and we're still learning.

Over these past 35 years, Christians of many backgrounds and traditions have shared with me their perspectives on the Israeli-Palestinian conflict, and there is an immense amount of literature on the subject. While I will seek to be as objective as possible, my own experiences have inevitably influenced my perspective.

1. The Ottoman Empire and the British Mandate

The Ottoman Empire, under Turkish domination, governed Palestine for 400 years, from 1517 to 1917. After World War I, the League of Nations was founded and the British were entrusted with the Mandate of Palestine. Before the Mandate began, the Balfour Declaration of November 2, 1917, had indicated the British readiness to favor a homeland for the Jewish people. It said:

> His Majesty's Government view with favour the establishment in Palestine of a national home for the Jewish people, and will use their best endeavours to facilitate the achievement of this object, it being clearly understood that nothing shall be done which may prejudice the civil and religious rights of existing non-Jewish communities in Palestine, or the rights and political status enjoyed by Jews in any other country.[1]

This official statement was a factor which led later to the United Nations' vote in November 1947 to divide Mandatory Palestine into two entities and make Jerusalem an international city belonging to everyone.

2. The Holocaust and the Birth of Israel

When the State of Israel was proclaimed by David Ben Gurion on May 15, 1948, the armies of the neighbor Arab countries all invaded the new-born nation. At its birth, Israel had a population of 660,000. Just three years earlier, World War II had ended. Nazi Germany had been defeated, and the Allied armies opened the gates of the concentration camps to discover the horrors of the Holocaust. Between 1939 and 1945, over 6,000,000 Jews and many others had been put to death in the most horrible and deliberate genocide in Nazi concentration camps. People always say that you cannot understand modern Israel unless you see it against the backdrop of the Holocaust when Jews had no way to defend themselves.

Everywhere in Israel, people still feel the continuing impact of the Holocaust. I remember the day in a Hebrew class I was attending when we were learning vocabulary which would enable us to understand interviews with Holocaust survivors on radio and television. In our notebooks we wrote the words in Hebrew for "concentration camp", "prison guard", "gas chamber", "crematorium". When time for a break came, the teacher, Ruth, came over to speak to Rivka, who sat next to me, on whose arm I had noticed a tattooed number. The tattoo revealed that Rivka was a survivor of a Nazi concentration camp. Ruth said to Rivka, "I know you were in one of the concentration camps. Do you mind if I ask you which one?"

Rivka replied, "I was in Auschwitz."

Ruth responded, "That's interesting, because my grandparents were both in Auschwitz; they were gassed and then put into the crematorium."

Rivka, visibly moved, said, "My older brother and sister, mother and father were also in Auschwitz and died the same way." Then they both started to cry.

Ruth then asked, "Do you mind if I ask how old you were at the time?"

Rivka replied, "I was 17." About the only way that a 17 year-old Jewish girl survived was because Nazi guards sexually abused her rather than kill her.

Across the years, we met a number of survivors of the Holocaust without actively searching for them, and their stories touched our lives. Israel's obsession with security and being able to defend oneself is understandable in the light of the Holocaust, which was preceded by almost 2,000 years of anti-semitism expressed in massacres, pogroms, and expulsions. Tragically, these events were most often carried out by people who called themselves "Christian", and were provoked by the anti-Jewish teaching of churches.

The reality of the Holocaust evoked support for the United Nations' vote that partitioned Mandatory Palestine. Many Christians in Western Europe and North America felt the guilt of what so-called "Christians" had done, or allowed to be done to the Jewish people. As a result, many committed themselves to support Israel from the time of its birth, and continue to do so enthusiastically. For some, this commitment has involved a rejection of all forms of evangelism. They asserted that, while the churches can never atone for providing the seedbed that led to the Holocaust, the presence and silent witness of Christians in support of Israel can at least bear witness to a different type of Christianity.[2]

From my first weeks in Jerusalem, I became aware that Christians are often polarized in their attitude toward the State of Israel. I recall being in a Palestinian Christian home in East Jerusalem when I encountered real anger from my host.

> We're sorry about what happened to the Jews in Europe, but it wasn't *our* fault. Why do we have to pay for the guilt you western Christians feel? What right do those Jews have to come here and take our land? Furthermore, we can't understand you western Christians. *We* are your fellow Christians. We have persevered in our faith in Christ since the first century. We have kept our faith across the centuries, even though many Christians were martyred by Muslim conquerors. Then you come from the West and say our land belongs to the Jews, and you don't identify with us, your fellow Christians! Doesn't the Bible talk about justice? What is the justice in what has happened to us Christian Arabs?

Arab Christians call the birth of Israel, "the great catastrophe". Many thousands of Arabs—both Christians and Muslims—lost their homes and properties, and were never compensated. Many thousands died, and hundreds of thousands became refugees in 1948-49.

Naim Ateek, a Palestinian Christian, came from the Arab village of Beisan, which was located right next to the ancient tell Beit She'an, a biblical city. On May 26, 1948, when he was a little boy, his town came under Israeli control, and he and his family and many others were forced at gun point to leave. His father, a goldsmith, begged to stay, but was told, "If you don't get out, we will kill you," so they became refugees near Nazareth.[3] They were never compensated for their property, on which a branch of *Bank Le'umi* stands today. Similar experiences happened to thousands of Christian or Muslim Arabs.

Since 1948, 531 Arab villages have been either destroyed by bulldozers or occupied by Israeli residents despite U.S. resolutions calling for the rightful return of these homes and lands to their Arab owners. According to U.N. records in June 1999, about 3.6 million Palestinian refugees are the victims of Israel's nationhood.[4] It should also be said that many thousands of Jewish refugees, survivors of the Holocaust or residents of predominantly Arab Muslim nations, found a safe home in Israel. They often arrived with only a simple suitcase.

3. After the war of 1948-49, the Wars of 1956 and 1967

In 1949 the fighting stopped, and an armistice was signed, but not a peace treaty. In 1956, when threatened by Egypt, the Israeli Defense Forces swept across the Sinai Peninsula to the Suez Canal. Under great pressure from the United States and Great Britain, Israel withdrew back to the borders of the 1949 armistice. United Nations forces were established on the border between Egypt and Israel to assure that fighting did not restart.

In 1967, President Nasser of Egypt demanded that the United Nation Truce Observation troops be removed from Sinai, including along the border with Israel, and daily announced on the radio that Israel would be pushed into the sea. With the first rays of the sun on a morning in June 1967, in a pre-emptive strike, Israeli planes destroyed most of the Egyptian and Syrian air force planes. Since Egyptian and Syrian ground troops then had little protective cover, the Israeli army quickly retook the Sinai Peninsula and the Golan Heights which Syria had controlled. When Jordan became involved in the conflict, the Israeli army took East Jerusalem, the Old City, and all of the area west of the Jordan River which had been under Jordanian control.

This became known as "the Six Day War" because of the length of time that the war lasted. In the months that followed, the United Nations Security Council debated the important wording of a resolution that continues to be re-emphasized—*Resolution 242,* which was approved on November 22, 1967. The following are its most important elements:

> The Security Council, *Expressing* its continuing concern with the grave situation in the Middle East, *Emphasizing* the inadmissibility of the acquisition of territory by war and the need to work for a just and lasting peace in which every State in the area can live in security, *Emphasizing* further that all Member States in their acceptance of the Charter of the United Nations have undertaken a commitment to act in accordance with Article 2 of the Charter, Affirms that the fulfilment of Charter principles requires the establishment of a just and lasting peace in the Middle East which should include the application of both the following principles:

> Withdrawal of Israeli armed forces from territories occupied in the recent conflict; Termination of all claims or states of belligerency and respect for and acknowledgement of the sovereignty, territorial integrity and political independence of every State in the area and their right to live in peace within secure and recognized boundaries free from threats or acts of force;

> Affirms further the necessity...for achieving a just settlement of the refugee problem[5]

The phrases which have been the focus of continuing debate are: "the inadmissibility of the acquisition of territory by war", "withdrawal of Israeli armed forces from territories occupied in the recent conflict", and "termination of all...belligerency". Palestinians say that Israel must withdraw from occupied territories, while Israel says it has not fulfilled those requirements because the Palestinians and Syrians have not fulfilled their obligation to end the state of belligerency and acknowledge Israel's sovereignty. This resolution continues to be foundational for all future possible negotiations.

The results of the 1967 War had a profound impact on Christians of different backgrounds. To those who supported Israel, it was a miracle of God. They looked at the map realizing that all of the area from the Jordan River to the Mediterranean Sea was now under Israeli control and drew comparisons with periods in biblical Israel's history when that same area was under the control of the Davidic and Solomonic Monarchy. Many evangelical authors wrote that biblical prophecy had been fulfilled, citing the prophetic words of Jeremiah, Ezekiel and Zechariah about the return of the Jewish people from exile.[6] Those who embraced a dispensational interpretation of Scripture increasingly saw the stage of history being prepared for the "Great Tribulation", the battle of Armageddon, and the Second Coming of Christ. They believed that Israel was to play a key role in the unfolding of these events.

Christian Arabs viewed the 1967 conflict in very different ways, with profound sorrow and discouragement, since now several million Palestinians had come under Israeli military occupation in the West Bank and the Gaza Strip.

4. The "Yom Kippur War" of 1973 and the Peace Treaty with Egypt

I was living in Jerusalem on *Yom Kippur* (the Day of Atonement) in October of 1973 when suddenly I heard air raid sirens. Most Israeli Jews were in their synagogues, for this is the one day of the year when even non-observant Jews attend synagogue and fast for 24 hours. The radio announced that Israel was being invaded by Syrian forces on the Golan Heights and that the Egyptian Army had crossed the Suez Canal and overrun the Israeli defenses there. Israeli intelligence had failed to discover the carefully planned effort to reclaim land lost by the Egyptians and Syrians in the War of 1967.

For about a week, the Egyptians and Syrians regained land in Sinai and in the Golan Heights, but finally the Israeli forces pushed them back. The Egyptian Fourth Army was completely surrounded on the eastern side of the Suez Canal in Sinai, while some of the Israeli army had crossed the Suez and held ground on the west side of the Canal. Henry Kissinger, the U. S. Secretary of State, went to Moscow and obtained the support of the Soviet government to call for a cease-fire in the UN Security Council. On October 22, 1973, the Security Council unanimously passed *Resolution 338,* calling for a cease-fire, negotiations, and the implementation of Resolution 242.[7] This was followed by a disengagement of forces, a return to the 1967 borders and the freeing of the Egyptian Fourth Army.

One significant factor of the War of 1973 was that the Hashemite Kingdom of Jordan did not participate in the invasion of Israel to seek to regain land lost in the War of 1967.

Subsequently, President Anwar Sadat of Egypt, having tried unsuccessfully to regain lost territory militarily, came to believe that Allah wanted him to take a different approach. He moved to recognize the existence of Israel and to undertake a dialogue in the hope of regaining Sinai through diplomatic efforts. I will never forget the euphoria when his plane landed in Tel Aviv and was welcomed by all the Israeli leadership. When we saw him in Jerusalem, he was visiting the Church of the Holy Sepulcher (called the "Church of the Resurrection" by the Greeks). He worshipped in the El Aqsa Mosque, the third most holy place in Islam, and gave an address in the Israeli Knesset (or Parliament). People were thrilled and filled with hope. Was it really happening?!

U. S. President Jimmy Carter brought President Anwar Sadat and Israeli Prime Minister Menahem Begin to Camp David where the components of a major agreement were hammered out. On March 27, 1979, the Peace Treaty between Israel and Egypt was signed on the lawn of the American White House.[8] In the months that followed, the Israeli Army withdrew from the Sinai Peninsula in stages. Israeli settlements that had been built in Northern Sinai were evacuated amidst strong opposition from the settlers and their supporters, but Israel kept its agreement.

On October 6, 1981, Egyptian President Anwar Sadat was assassinated while on the reviewing stand of a victory parade.[9] Members of the Muslim Brotherhood, who had vehemently opposed the peace with Israel, were found to be responsible and were brought to justice. Despite many tensions and disagreements, it is amazing that Israel and Egypt still have diplomatic relations and that it is possible to travel between the two countries.

Meanwhile, what was happening with the Palestinians? Sadat had sought to bring representative Palestinians into the negotiations, but they refused, and Menahem Begin did not want any talk of "independence" for Palestinians. At that time, the major term in diplomatic discussions was "autonomy" for the Palestinians, but there was no implementation of such a hope.

5. Israeli Settlements in the West Bank and Gaza; 1982 Invasion of Lebanon and Oslo Peace Accords

During our first years in Israel/Palestine, it was easy to travel throughout the West Bank and into Gaza. There were few roadblocks and we were seldom stopped, even for a check of documents. Then the Israeli government started a policy of planting settlements for Jewish citizens in the territories taken during the 1967 War. Many of the settlers were religiously motivated, believing that God had promised them the land. They said they were establishing homes in "Judea and Samaria," which were the names for that geographical area during the Second Temple Period, or what Christians would call the New Testament period. Some settlements like Shiloh (I Samuel 1:3-28; 3:21, etc.) were intentionally built on or near the archaeological site of the biblical town. Likewise, secular Jews were often settlers, but they asserted that Israel needed the West Bank and Gaza for security, since their neighboring countries had repeatedly refused to recognize Israel and have direct negotiations with them.

The settlements multiplied and grew, and Palestinians viewed this as discriminatory and unjust. One issue was water, which was provided by pipelines connected to the Israeli settlements, but not to Palestinian villages. Palestinian requests for permits to dig new wells were rejected without reason. Also, as settlers' demands grew, more Palestinian land was confiscated or expropriated, with no compensation given. New roads were built and paved to the settlements, but Palestinians were generally refused permission to drive on them. Olive groves, long a major source of income to Palestinian farmers, were confiscated and bulldozed. Palestinian anger grew as the military occupation of their land continued and there was no progress politically toward the creation of a Palestinian state.

Messianic Jews, who believe in Jesus as Messiah, often supported Israeli settlements on the West Bank, claiming, with religious Jews, that God had promised them the Land and that they were simply taking possession of their biblical heritage. Palestinian Christians, on the other hand, increasingly shared the anger and frustration of their Muslim neighbors because of the suffering and discrimination.

Just north of Israel lies *Lebanon* where many thousands of Palestinians lived in squalor as refugees.[10] The Palestine Liberation Organization (PLO), under Yasser Arafat, had been training guerila fighters who made occasional forays into northern Israel. On June 6, 1982, Israel launched a massive invasion into Lebanon with the announced purpose of destroying the PLO, since its charter from 1968 had expressed the goal of liquidating Israel. The Israeli army went all the way to Beirut, ultimately forcing Arafat to flee to Tunisia to establish a new base. Israeli forces finally withdrew, except for a "security zone" of about fifteen kilometers above its northern border. In 2000, under then Prime Minister Ehud Barak, all Israeli forces withdrew south of the border, ending the occupation of that security zone.

A glimmer of hope for peace emerged in September 1993, when it was revealed that Israeli and Palestinian negotiators had been meeting secretly in Oslo, Norway, and had come to an agreement of principles. Israel and the PLO agreed to mutual recognition, the PLO promised to change its charter and Israel promised to withdraw from select Palestinian urban centers and permit the establishment of a Palestinian Authority.[11]

On September 28, 1995, Prime Minister Yitzhak Rabin and Chairman Yasser Arafat of the PLO signed the Israeli-Palestinian Interim Agreement on the West Bank and the Gaza Strip in Washington, D.C. in the presence of U.S. President Bill Clinton, King Hussein of Jordan, and representatives of Egypt and the European Union.[12] Tragically, the hope was short-lived, since on November 4, 1995, just six weeks after the signing, a right-wing Israeli radical assassinated Prime Minister Yitzhak Rabin.

6. Suicide Bombers, Expanding Settlements, and Christian interpretations

A serious new development in the Israeli-Palestinian conflict developed in the early 1990's, as young Palestinian Muslims strapped on explosives under their clothing, and became human bombs, committing suicide while trying to kill as many Israeli Jews as possible. These suicide bombers exploded on busses, in restaurants, and various other settings. There was a terrible toll in human life and destruction.

"Palestinians have killed over a thousand Israelis in terror and suicide attacks," it was reported. "Israelis have killed over 3,500 Palestinians in 'defense' operations and reprisals, including many civilians. The Intifada destroyed the belief of many Israelis in the possibility of peace, and destroyed the credibility of Yasser Arafat and the PLO as peace partners. Israeli retaliation and repression further embittered the Palestinians."[13]

It is significant that to date no Christian has been a suicide bomber. One Palestinian Christian organization, *Sabeel,* headed by Dr. Naim Ateek (quoted above on p. 16), devoted a special issue of its publication, *CornerStone*, to this phenomenon. In the lead article entitled: "Suicide Bombers: What is theologically and morally wrong with suicide bombings? A Palestinian Christian perspective,"[14] Dr. Ateek writes, "As a Christian, I know that the way of Christ is the way of non-violence, and therefore, I condemn all forms of violence and terrorism whether coming from the government of Israel or from militant Palestinian groups."[15] At the same time, the publication seeks to help people understand the underlying causes of the bombings, citing "the oppressive Israeli occupation, unemployment and confinement, imprisonment and torture, hopelessness, racism, discrimination, as well as other reasons."[16]

Christians supporting Israel have a very different emphasis and interpretation of what has happened. They do not focus on Palestinian suffering, but on Israel which, they say, must be supported since it constantly faces the attacks of other terrorists. Their focus is on prophecy and its fulfillment. The birth of Israel as a nation, and the Israeli victory of 1967 are viewed as significant steps in preparation for the Second Coming of Christ. The website www.armegeddon. com, the world's largest selection of books on biblical prophecy, lists 900 titles, many of which espouse this interpretation of events in the Middle East. The best known author who has popularized this dispensational interpretation is Hal Lindsey, author, with C.C. Carlson, of *The Late Great Planet Earth,* (1970), which has sold over 35,000,000 copies. Lindsey asserts that three things must happen before the Second Coming of Christ: 1) Israel had to be reborn in the land of Palestine; 2) the Jews were to "repossess Old Jerusalem and the sacred sites, and 3) they would rebuild their ancient temple of worship on its historic site."[17] While Lindsey recognizes that that site is where the Dome of the Rock presently stands in Jerusalem, and that this is an "obstacle", he confidently declares, "Obstacle or no obstacle, it is certain that the Temple will be rebuilt. Prophecy demands it."[18] Prophecy, it seems, is understood as a *predestined* series of events in which Israel plays a key role, but in which Palestinian concerns for justice are never addressed.

Christian Zionism generally encompasses the position of many Christians who give strong and unequivocal support to Israel politically. It tends to build its case on the way it interprets Scripture. While many authors reveal that dispensational interpretation is the dominant hermeneutic among Christian Zionists, others, like David Parsons of the International Christian Embassy Jerusalem, emphasize that their support is built on their understanding of Covenantal Theology.[19]

7. "Intifada", Peace Negotiations, and a High Wall

In the early 1990's, Palestinians expressed their anger and outrage with the military occupation by what was called the "intifada" or "intifadeh", Arabic for "uprising".

After the Oslo Accords and the agreement to work toward a two-state solution to the conflict, the Palestinian Authority (PA) was established, and the Israeli Army withdrew from some Palestinian urban centers in the West Bank.

Even with the adoption of the Oslo Interim Agreements, the expansion of Jewish *settlements in the West Bank* has never stopped. A very few unauthorized settlement outposts have been disbanded, but in the meantime, "Israel continued to expand settlements throughout the peace process that began in 1993 and continues to do so today."[20] It is estimated that there are 220,000 Jewish settlers living in the West Bank. For many Palestinian Christians, the settlements and the settlers represent a major obstacle to any kind of resolution of the conflict.

In July 2000, U.S. President Bill Clinton brought President Yasser Arafat and Prime Minister Ehud Barak to Camp David for further negotiations. While they reached agreement in some important areas, ultimately the negotiations broke down over the status of Jerusalem, and a decision about the return of Palestinian refugees or their compensation for loss and property.

On September 28, 2000, Israeli Prime Minister Ariel Sharon, with a large contingent of military and police, "visited" what Jews call the "Temple Mount", and Arabs call the "Haram Es Sharif", the third most holy site in Islam. This provocative act led to the eruption of Palestinian violence and what became known as the "Second Intifada." The Israeli Army was quick to respond, re-entering the cities of the West Bank. In Ramallah, the *de facto* seat of the Palestinian Authority, all the fledgling beginnings of Palestinian statehood (in the Departments of Education, Health Services, Interior, Foreign Affairs), were destroyed: computer and communication systems, records were smashed, or thrown out of windows. PA President Arafat was surrounded and isolated in his office. Other cities, such as Bethlehem, were re-entered and put under brutal curfews, which entailed closing down stores and schools, except for brief periods.

Suicide bombers continued their killing and destruction, and this finally led the Israeli government to begin construction of a *wall*, also called the "security barrier", "apartheid wall" or "separation wall", built inside the West Bank. In some places it cuts deeply into the West Bank to insure that certain large Jewish settlements will be on the Israeli side. Palestinians claim that, from their perspective, it is a pretext to confiscate more of their land. In many places, it separates Palestinian farmers from their land and from other towns. Pupils can no longer reach their schools, or they have to go a long distance around and through an intimidating checkpoint with long delays. Under international pressure, the route has been modified several times. It is twice the height of the Berlin Wall. The International Court of Justice declared the wall or barrier to be in violation of international law. Israel claims that because the number of suicide bombings has decreased significantly since its construction, it demonstrates the legitimacy of having the wall, i.e., it is saving Israeli lives.

8. A Future Palestinian State?

Can there be, or should there be a future *Palestinian State?* Mainstream Palestinians continue to demand a state in the West Bank and Gaza. But what kind of state would it be? Israeli settlement blocks have their own connecting roads, but Palestinian cities and villages are like islands, and their road links are increasingly difficult to navigate due to Israeli roadblocks. A Palestinian state would be like disconnected "Bantustans", such as those proposed under South Africa's apartheid system.

Christian Zionists oppose a two-state solution to the conflict, that is the State of Israel along side of a Palestinian state composed of the West Bank and Gaza. They also oppose negotiations which would give up Israeli military control over any land west of the Jordan River. Along with that position, they support the continuation of building Jewish settlements. In these issues they identify with the far right in Israeli politics. They claim that Jordan is a "Palestinian State" because of the high percentage of the population which originated in Palestine.[21] Meanwhile, Palestinian Christian organizations like *Sabeel* are strong advocates of a two state solution.[22]

In August 2005, Israel forcibly removed all of its settlers from the Gaza strip and handed over all its settlements there to Palestinians. This *disengagement,* featuring withdrawal of the Israeli army, seemed to offer some hope of a model for the West Bank, but Palestinian radicals began to fire Qassam rockets into southern Israel, so the Israeli army has moved back repeatedly into Gaza to try to locate and stop the launching of the rockets. It no longer seems to be a helpful possible model for West Bank disengagement.

9. Christian responses to this painful history and present political realities

Within this historical overview, we have looked only briefly at the contrasting interpretations and commitments of Christians. There are Christians who support Israel because they feel they can do no other after the horror of the Holocaust. There are others who base their support on their interpretation of Scripture, believing that these are "the last days", in preparation for the Second Coming of Christ and the Battle of Armageddon. On the other hand, there are Christian Palestinians and their supporters who believe that God loves both peoples in the Land equally, and that God is the God of justice who identifies with the oppressed—which they identify as themselves. Should one interpret the birth of Israel as a fulfillment of biblical prophecy, or as a great "catastrophe"? Is Israel's claim to the Land to be affirmed or rejected as a gross injustice?

How shall we interpret Scripture as it relates to Israel? Can scriptural references to Israel, which occur with very different connotations, be directly applied to the State of Israel today? What hermeneutical principles are appropriate when dealing with prophecy? Is sufficient distinction made between *apocalyptic* and *prophetic* literature?

What role should Christians play who live outside of Israel/Palestine? Is it possible to support both peoples and contribute to reconciliation *and* peace with justice?

In the presentations which follow, these and other important questions will be addressed by representative Jewish and Arab voices from Israel/Palestine. As we listen, may God grant us the grace to hear with sensitivity and compassion and to base our responses on responsible interpretation of Scripture, and wise supportive action.

Endnotes

1   See the excellent Middle East website for documents: www.mideast-web.org/mebalfour.htm

2   The Christian *Moshav*, or cooperative settlement, Nes Amim in western Galilee is perhaps the best example of this. They primarily grow longstem roses which are shipped by air for sale in Europe, and thus help the economy. Residents, mainly from Holland, Germany, and Switzerland, reject evangelism, but seek to be a Christian presence and learn from Judaism.

3   Naim S. Ateek, "An Arab-Israeli's Theological Reflections on the State of Israel after 40 Years," lecture given to the Ecumenical Theological Research Fraternity in Israel, Feb. 25, 1988, p. 2.

4   J. Fayex, *Lest the Civilized World Forget: The Colonization of Palestine* (New York: Americans for Middle East Understanding, 1992). Has a catalog of the villages.

5   Quoted from www.mideastweb.org/242.htm, where the full resolution may be found.

6   Some of the passages most frequently quoted are Jeremiah 16:15; 23:3,8; 24:6; 29:14; 32:37,40, Ezekiel 11:17; 20:34,41; 36:28; 37:21,25; 39:25-28, etc. Some exegetes ask if these promises of return to the Land were fulfilled after the Babylonian exile, at least in part. Others speak of "double fulfillment." See Michael J. Pragai, *Faith and Fulfillment: Christians and the Return to the Promised Land,* (London: Vallentine, Mitchell, 1985)

7   www.mideastweb.org/338.htm. The website www.mideastweb.org gives excellent, balanced summaries of the history of the Israeli-Palestinian conflict. Other references from the website follow.

8   www.mideastweb.org/egyptisraeltreaty.htm

9   www.mideastweb.org/timeline.htm

10   Many Palestinian refugees had crossed into Jordan in 1948 or 1967, but when fighting began in Jordan, they fled into southern Lebanon. In that context they joined the PLO in hopes of "liberating" Palestine.

11   www.meweb.org/meoslodop.htm

12   www.meweb.org/mesoint.htm

13   www.mideastweb.org/briefhistory.htm

14   Naim Ateek, "Suicide Bombers: What is theologically and morally wrong with suicide bombings? A Palestinian Christian perspective." *CornerStone,* Issue 25, Summer 2002, (Jerusalem: Sabeel), pp. 1-5.

> *Sabeel* "is an ecumenical grassroots liberation theology movement among Palestinian Christians. Inspired by the life and teachings of Jesus Christ...*Sabeel* strives to develop a spirituality based on justice, peace, non-violence, liberation, and reconciliation for the different national & faith communities."

15   *Ibid.,* p. 1.

16   *Ibid.,* p. 3.

17   Hal Lindsey with C.C. Carlson, *The Late Great Planet Earth,* (Grand Rapids: Zondervan, 1970) p. 40.

18   *Ibid,* p. 45.

19   David Parsons, "Swords into Ploughshares: Christian Zionism and the Battle of Armageddon", especially Section 2, "Covenantal Theology: the Foundation of Biblical Zionism", website of International Christian Embassy Jerusalem. www.icej.org/data/images/file/news/swords.pdf

20   www.mideastweb.org/briefhistory.htm#modern%20history

21   See www.christianactionforisrael.org for well-stated articles presenting Christian Zionism.

22   See www.sabeel.org for statements of purpose and positions taken at their conferences.

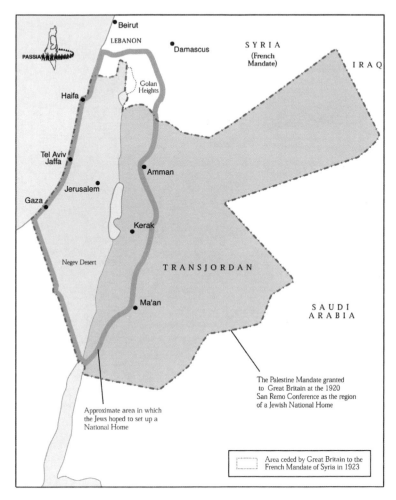

Fig. 3.1: Palestine under the British Mandate 1923-1948.

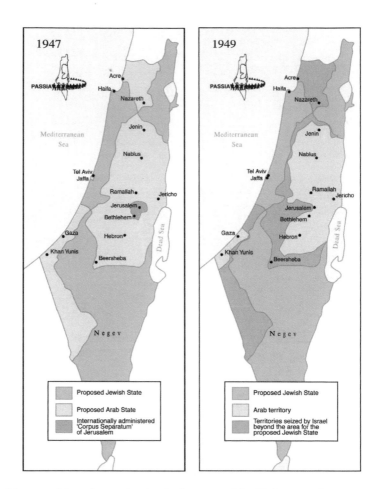

Fig. 3.2: Moved to action by the horrors of the Holocaust, the UN votes to divide Palestine into Jewish and Arab states. Jerusalem, it says, will belong to the world. Arab nations attack after Israel declares independence in May 1948, spawning the Palestinian refugee crisis. Israel wins the war and territory before the armistice in 1949 at Rhodes. Copyright Palestinian Academic Society for the Study of International Affairs. Used by permission.

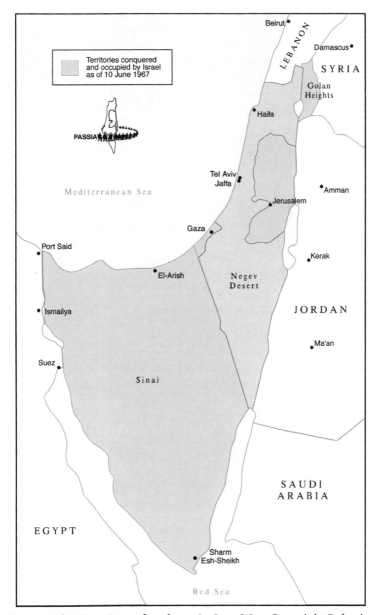

*Fig. 3.3: The Near East after the 1967 June War. Copyright Palestin-
ian Academic Society for the Study of International Affairs.
Used by permission.*

Fig. 3.4: The Golan Heights. Copyright Palestinian Academic Society for the Study of International Affairs. Used by permission.

Fig. 3.5: Oslo II. This map reveals the problem of trying to create a
Palestinian state on disconnected pieces of land, separated
often by Israeli settlements and roads built "for Israeli vehi-
cles only." Copyright Palestinian Academic Society for the
Study of International Affairs. Used by permission.

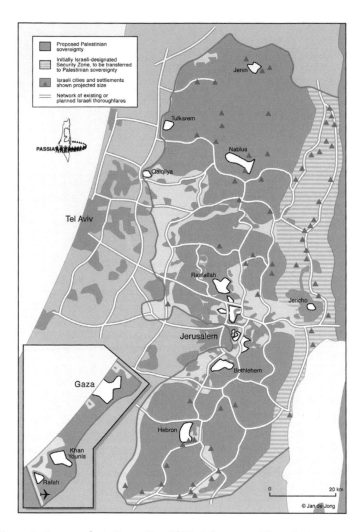

Fig. 3.6: Proposal at Camp David II, July 2000. Negotiations in summer 2000, of which President Clinton was the host, break down over Jerusalem and the rights of Palestinian refugees. This shows the proposed division of sovereignty in the West Bank, presented by Israel. Copyright Palestinian Academic Society for the Study of International Affairs. Used by permission.

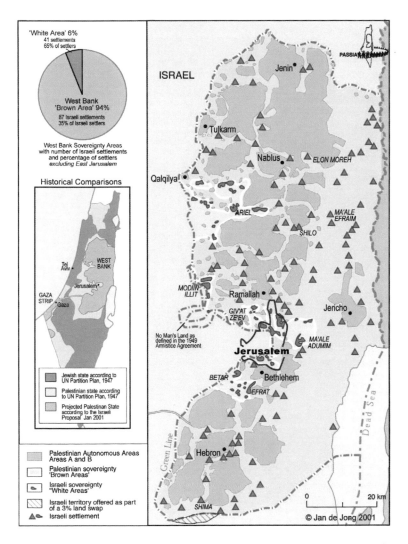

Fig. 3.7: Final Status Map Presented by Israel, January 2001. Copyright Palestinian Academic Society for the Study of International Affairs. Used by permission.

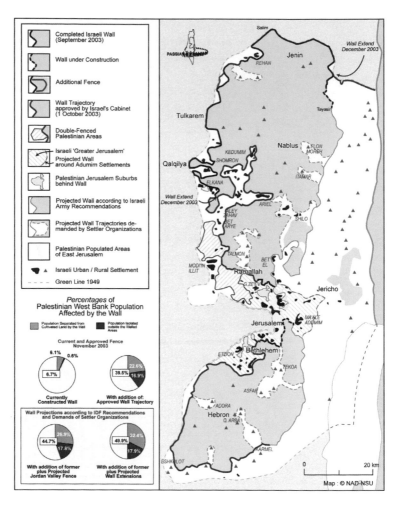

Fig. 3.8: Israel's Separation Barrier or Wall, built to prevent suicide bombers from entering Israel, actually separates Palestinians from large areas of their agricultural land and facilitates taking more West Bank land for Israeli settlements. Copyright Foundation for Middle East Peace. Used by permission.

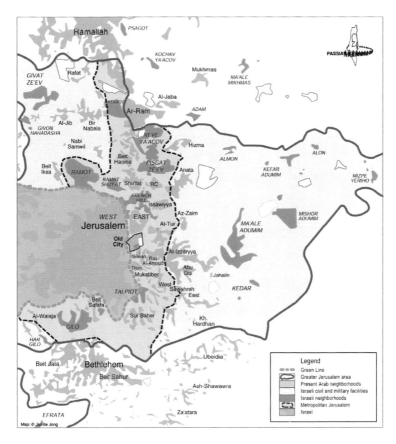

Fig. 3.9: Greater Jerusalem. Copyright Palestinian Academic Society for the Study of International Affairs. Used by permission.

Fig. 3.10: The Wall, shown where it intersects Bethany, just east of Jerusalem, is 8 meters (about 26 ft.) high and closes the main road used by Palestinians from Jerusalem to Jericho. It divides Palestinians from Palestinians and Palestinians from Israelis. Israel says it is needed for security. Photo by Rev. Alex Awad.

Fig. 3.11: Israeli Messianic youth join hands with Palestinian Christian youth symbolically on a rock bridge during a desert camping encounter sponsored by Musalaha, a ministry of reconciliation in Israel/Palestine. See pp. 152-153, 158.

4

Messianic Jewish Views on Israel's Rebirth and Survival in the Light of Scripture

LISA LODEN

It has frequently been said that wherever you have two Jews you will have three opinions. Messianic Jews are no exception to this rather humorous indictment. There are, however, a small number of issues on which the vast majority of Messianic Jews find themselves substantially in agreement. This is the case with the subject of this paper. Although some of the positions held are more nuanced than others, the general trajectory is that the rebirth of Israel as a nation and her subsequent survival, have come about and will continue by divine intervention in history.

In many forums of discussion, the term "rebirth" is frequently used in relation to Israel, the usual understanding being that the modern geopolitical state of Israel is implied. This use therefore weights the discussion towards political considerations. As the issue being dealt with here is primarily theological, the preferred term is "restoration." Rebirth occurs as a one-time event and restoration is an ongoing process encompassing both rebirth and survival. This paper will speak in terms of restoration rather than rebirth. In both Christian and Jewish circles, the term restoration has a lengthy history. In Jewish circles, the term has been used continuously and in Christianity, it has been in use at least since the time of the Puritans. Among both Jews and Christians, there is a long tradition of hope and expectation for Israel to be restored. Concerning the 20th century phenomena of the resurgence of the nation state of Israel "restoration" is the commonly used term.

The purpose of this paper is to elucidate the various views that are commonly held by the Messianic Jewish community regarding the restoration of Israel. No attempt will be made to critique these views, but simply to present them for consideration. Messianic Jews acknowledge that scripture, both the Old and the New Testaments, are the authoritative basis for their life and theology. This paper will also examine the interpretive grids through which Messianic Jews view scripture and arrive at their understandings.

At first glance the subject appears to be straightforward. However, upon further consideration the picture is not so clear. Terminology is ambiguous and definitions need to be agreed upon. This presents a multitude of difficulties, not the least of which is identifying just who or what Israel is. Is Israel the Jewish people, the modern nation-state, the territory, is it a spiritual category or a physical entity or is it both? The reality is that scripture uses the word "Israel" in a variety of ways. Yohanna Katanacho notes that,

> ...the word "Israel" is mentioned more than 2500 times in the OT and more than 73 times in the NT. The NT uses this word to refer to several things:
>
> 1) the house of Jacob (Matt. 8: 10; 10: 6);
>
> 2) the land of Israel (Matt. 2: 20; 10: 23; Lk. 4: 27);
>
> 3) the servant of God (Lk. 1: 54);
>
> 4) the Church (Rom. 9: 6; Gal. 6: 16); and
>
> 5) the Northern Kingdom (Heb. 8: 8).
>
> Moreover, the OT adds to our list other meanings, such as:
>
> 1) Jacob;

2) all the Transjordanian tribes without the tribes in Cisjordan (Josh. 22: 13);

3) all the tribes in Transjordan except Benjamin (Judges 20: 1, 3);

4) the United Kingdom; and

5) different borders during the period of the divided kingdom.

This confusion in terminology becomes more complex when people equate the State of Israel with the house of Jacob. They overlook several factors:

1) More than 20% of the citizens of the State of Israel are not Jews;

2) Many Jews around the world are not Israelis;

3) 50% of those who live in the land of Israel/Palestine are not Jews;

4) Some Jews are converts and are not biological Jews (Est. 8: 17);

5) Some Jewish families have become Christians or Muslims.[1]

For the Messianic Jew, however, Israel is ethnic Israel. Israel is always the Jewish people whether they reside in the modern state of Israel or if they live outside of the geopolitical boundaries of the nation state. For Messianic Jews, the survival of Israel is axiomatic.

Because of the centrality of Israel in God's plan...Messianic Jews are ardent Zionists. They support Israel because the Jewish State is viewed as a direct fulfillment of biblical prophecy. Although Israel is far from perfect, Messianic Jews believe that God is active in the history of the nation and that the Jews will never be driven out of their land again.[2]

How Israel survives, physically or spiritually or both, whether enjoying unqualified covenant blessing or undergoing judgment prior to blessing, remains a matter of debate.

1. Restoration as Fulfillment

The statement of faith of the Messianic Jewish Alliance of America, an association of congregations, says:

> We believe in God's end-time plan for the nation of Israel and for the world. A central part of Messianic Judaism is the belief in the physical and spiritual restoration of Israel, as taught in the Scriptures. The greatest miracle of our day has been the re-establishment or rebirth of the State of Israel according to prophecy (Ezek. 34:11-31, 36-39; Hos. 3; Amos 9:11-15; Zech. 12-14, Isa. 11, 43, 54, 60-62, 66; Rom. 11:1-34).[3]

Israeli Messianic voices echo these sentiments. Joseph Shulam, a prominent Messianic leader, writes:

> God gave the land of Israel to the seed of Abraham forever. He promised to bring Israel back to the Land after her exile among the nations. (cf. Isa. 37, 39:23ff., Isa. 60-61). Israel is at present seeing the fulfillment of these promises.[4]

A Messianic Jew who lives in Israel often sees his presence in that land as both fulfillment of prophecy and as an eschatological sign. The Messianic Jew's identity is integrally related to being a part of the Jewish people who have returned to the promised land to fulfill their final destiny. Although there are a number of different views as to the sequence of events in the end-times, there is almost universal agreement that **these** times are the times of the end.

> Finally, Isaiah 51:10 says that 'the redeemed of the Lord shall return and come with singing unto Zion and everlasting joy shall be upon their head.' If these 'redeemed of the Lord' are not the Messianic Jews now living in the Land, then who are they?'[5]

This view has been a part of the Messianic Jewish consciousness since before the foundation of the modern state of Israel. Messianic Jews (then called Hebrew Christians) were involved in political Zionist movements in Europe. Their involvement was based on their understanding of the prophetic scriptures concerning the return of Israel to Zion.

> Those Hebrew Christians who enthusiastically expressed Zionist aspirations, in word or in deed, did so from an inherent belief rooted in their understanding of biblical prophecy. In fact, their Zionism, which often integrated political and spiritual aspects, should be understood as a conditio sine qua non of their individual and national identity. ...

> In the idea of Zion's restoration there was the expectancy of a further fulfillment of human history within the framework of the history of man's redemption. ...Zionism was 'ordained' to pave the way physically for the movement of the dry bones (Ezek. 38) leading into a spiritual renaissance.[6]

In this respect, little has changed and Messianic Jews today continue to embrace a Zionist agenda.

2. Messianic Jewish use of Scripture

Messianic Jews consistently maintain the Jewishness of the biblical documents (understandably of course the Old Testament but equally the Jewishness of the New Testament is heavily emphasized) and some advocate the use of traditional rabbinic approaches to hermeneutics and exposition. The fact that "Rabbinic interpretation is in large measure founded on the assumption that Scripture contains potentially unlimited meaning"[7] allows for an exceptionally varied approach to the interpretation of scripture in certain quarters of the Messianic movement. It should nonetheless be noted that there is no consensus among Messianic Jews regarding the use of rabbinic sources and interpretation.[8]

The question of single or multiple meanings of scripture is an important issue and there are a variety of views on the subject. Dan Juster, a prominent spokesman and theologian of the Messianic Jewish movement, is sensitive to this issue. Juster exhibits a thorough grasp of evangelical biblical interpretation but he is in continuity with the Jewish approach when he writes,

> One meaning is capable of multiple applications...I hold to a more charismatic and prophetic approach whereby the Holy Spirit gives new applications and jumping off points, but never in a replacement of the original author's intended meaning.[9]

Few Messianic Jews have seriously addressed themselves to the matter of hermeneutics in biblical interpretation. This reflects the community's largely unquestioned view of scripture as being plain and incontestable and is particularly evident in regard to the restoration of Israel. A literal hermeneutic is decidedly the hermeneutic of choice by the overwhelming majority of Messianic Jews writing on the subject.

While accepting both the Old and the New Testaments as canon, authoritative and binding, Messianic Jews base their views of Israel's restoration on the prophetic scriptures of the Old Testament understood by means of a literal hermeneutic. Almost without exception the views of Messianic Jews concerning the restoration of Israel are argued from the Old Testament prophets.

There are a few notable exceptions to this in the North American Messianic camp. Mark Kinzer is one of these voices. Kinzer recognizes and states that,

> Many Messianic Jews consider the message of the Bible as clear and indisputable, a fact independent of external interpretation. The individual who reads the text with faith and an open heart will understand what it says.... (However,) All attempts at a purely biblical perspective are destined to fail. One never reads the biblical text apart from preconceptions drawn from one's own particular historical setting and from some stream of interpretive tradition. That setting and tradition will shape the questions we address to the text, the concepts and terms we use to answer those questions and our selection of the portions of the text that speak most directly to our questions and therefore seem to be of the greatest importance....[10]

Kinzer employs a canonical theological approach to biblical interpretation. He disassociates himself from the Evangelical Christian
world and finds an affinity with both Catholic and liberal Protestants
who are taking a new approach to Paul. Kinzer bases his arguments
regarding the spiritual and physical continuity of the Jewish people
on a rereading of the New Testament texts according to his canonical theological approach. His understanding of the importance of
history differs significantly from that of the majority of Messianic
Jews who write on the subject. Kinzer is anti-supercessionist, is
unequivocal concerning the survival of the Jewish people (Israel)
and argues for Messianic Jews in communion with non-believing
Jews as obligated to an observance of Jewish ceremonial law as a
prerequisite for the survival of the people of Israel.

> From a theological perspective, it is more reasonable to assume that
> God's commitment to the Jewish people and its distinctive way of life
> has been sustained throughout the past two millennia. This leads to
> rejection rather than revision of traditional supersessionism. Jews
> who have not believed in Yeshua but who have loyally sustained a
> continual Jewish communal presence in the world through the hours
> of deepest darkness are heirs of God's covenant with Israel. This
> view is consistent with the ...realities of the last two thousand years
> of history.... We are concerned at this point with the spiritual status
> of the Jewish people. How do we initially assess the historical reality
> of Jewish existence these past two millennia in the light of the New
> Testament, and (just as important) how do we read the New Testa-
> ment in the light of that historical reality?[11]

Kinzer's approach results in a theology of the continuity of Israel as
the Jewish people through history rather than a recent restoration.
More importantly, among Messianic Jews he is the lone voice that
engages extensively with New Testament texts.

An example of Kinzer's exegesis of Matthew 23:37-39 will illus-
trate this:

> ...Matthew assumes (1) that Jerusalem will be standing as a Jewish
> city before the return of Yeshua, (2) that its inhabitants (and all
> Jews) are still the beloved lost sheep of Israel, whose response to

God is crucial for the final redemption of the world and (3) that the conduct rather than the legitimacy of its leaders is rejected, since the response demanded in Matthew 23:39 is not just popular but also official.[12]

Although not without harsh critics, Kinzer's voice is important and is gaining influence in the Messianic Jewish world.

A typical mainstream Messianic Jewish approach to the question of the restoration of Israel is expressed by David Miller who unequivocally employs a literal hermeneutic in his article "Messianic Judaism and the Theology of the Land." He says:

> The history of the Jewish people begins with the call of Abraham... From that time the national and spiritual history of the Jewish people has been inseparably linked with the land of promise. Throughout the ages the Jewish people have believed that their presence in the land was a result of God's faithfulness to the covenant which he made with Abraham, and when they have been dispersed from the land they have been confident that this same faithfulness would someday restore them. The covenant which God made with Abraham was unconditional, irrevocable, and confirmed with an oath.[13]

Miller by no means stands alone in his understanding. These views are repeatedly expressed by Messianic Jews, whether or not they reside in Israel.[14]

Dr. David Stern, a Messianic Jew living in Israel, also employs a literal or 'plain sense' hermeneutic. He expresses his perspective in the following terms:

> The promise of the land of Israel is forever, and the plain sense of this is that the Jewish people will possess the land (at least in trusteeship) and live there. To say that the New Covenant transforms this plain sense into an assertion that those who believe in Yeshua come into some vague spiritual 'possession' or a spiritual 'territory' is intellectual slight of hand aiming at denying, canceling and reducing to naught a real promise given to a real people in the real world.[15]

One of the most prolific theologians of the current Messianic movement is Dr. Arnold Fructenbaum.[16] He was trained at Dallas Theological Seminary, is a classical dispensationalist and uses a literal or plain sense hermeneutic. In the introduction to his article "Eschatology and Messianic Jews: A Theological Perspective," Fructenbaum writes:

In dealing with this issue, sound hermeneutical principles have been applied. First, there is the principle of literal interpretation of Scripture. The normal plain sense is assumed rather than assuming a figurative, spiritual or allegorical meaning – unless the text itself indicates otherwise, Second this rejects the presuppositions of replacement theology in any of its forms and expressions. This means that at no point is the Church ever referred to as "Israel," or "Spiritual Israel," or some other term favored by replacement theologians. Of the seventy-three times the term "Israel is found in the New Testament – not once is it used of the Church. It is either used of Jews in general or Jewish believers in particular, but always of ethnic Jews and never of Gentiles or of the Church.

On the subject of Israel, the doctrinal statement of Fructenbaum's Ariel Ministries states:

We believe that God called a people to Himself who are the physical descendants of Abraham, Isaac, and Jacob; that Israel is the Wife of Jehovah, unfaithful in the past, divorced in the present, and to be reunited in the future; that God has made four unconditional covenants with this elect nation that have remained unfulfilled; that God intends to fulfill all His promises to Israel in a literal way just as His warnings and judgments were fulfilled in a literal way; that in Israel's history of unbelief there has always been a believing remnant according to the election of grace; that there will be a national regeneration.

3. Popular Understanding

Although the survey from which I will quote was taken ten years ago, the opinions of Messianic Jews have remained stable. The survey sought to ascertain the opinions of Messianic Jews living in the land of Israel, on subjects of Israel, the land, the people and the promises of God. It showed that an overwhelming 95% of those surveyed believe that the Bible clearly promises the land of Israel to the Jewish people.[17] Those surveyed represented a wide spectrum of theological persuasions, yet on the issue of the land of Israel being irrevocably the possession of the Jewish people there was almost absolute consensus.

One of the questions asked of the respondents was whether they believed that Zionism was God's tool to fulfill prophecies in the end times. Sixty-two percent of the women surveyed responded positively as did seventy-two percent of the men. Twenty percent of the women and twenty-five percent of the men were 'not sure.' This result shows that only eighteen percent of the women and three percent of the men *did not* believe that Zionism was God's tool to fulfill prophecies in the end times.[18] The respondents clearly saw this present time in history as the "end times."

Concerning the survival of Israel, one of the recurrent themes expressed by Messianic Jews is the expectation of opposition towards Israel and the Jewish people as a part of end-time scenarios. David Stern claims to speak for the majority of Messianic Jews in Israel:

> In this I think I can safely claim to speak for virtually all Messianic Jews in Israel. Zechariah 12 and 14 proclaim the day when all nations will come against Jerusalem and the Lord (that is, the Messiah Yeshua) will fight and defeat them. The Jewish people will be saved as they recognize and mourn for their Messiah, 'whom they have pierced' (Zechariah 12:10). He, the Messiah, will be standing on the Mount of Olives, 'with all his holy ones,' repelling and defeating all the nations battling the Jews.[19]

A variation of this view was expressed by several of the respondents in another survey taken by a Messianic journal in 2001. In response to the question, "As a believer do you see any special meaning in the violence that erupted at New Year, 2000?" one respondent answered:

> I certainly see what is happening now as the beginning of the end. The Palestinians, in my opinion, are part of the coalition of Gog and

Magog...The Palestinians, especially in their struggle for self deter-
mination, are inciting the whole world against Israel and are awakening it to join in a war to liberate Jerusalem. ... This is the last act in
the war of Islam against the truth of God. We as believers must see
our place in this reality, otherwise our existence has no meaning.[20]

It is clear from this response that the identity and meaning for
his existence as a Messianic Jew is inextricably tied to his understanding of Israel's restoration according to his interpretation of
the scriptures. This sentiment is frequently expressed by Messianic
Jews.

In answer to the same question, Daniel Yahav, a Messianic leader
from Tiberias, expresses a similar if more moderate view:

I see the current situation as part of a process. All that the Palestinians
are doing, not just now but from the beginning of the first intifada,
is meant to serve their purpose of enlisting, in stages, international
public opinion against Israel. The influence of this process is widen-
ing and deepening the image of Israel as Goliath and the Palestinians
as David. All of this serves to fulfill the picture that Zechariah paints
at the beginning of chapter 12 when he speaks about the day when all
of the nations will come up to fight against Jerusalem.[21]

4. Conclusion

Messianic Jews view the restoration of Israel as an indisputable
sign of God's involvement in history. For this community, Israel,
people and nation, is the particularized embodiment of God's faithfulness – first to Jewish people and then by extrapolation, to the
entire world. Israel's restoration is a fulfillment of prophetic scripture and is an eschatological sign of the return of the Lord and the
end of history.

This paper has attempted to demonstrate that most, if not all,
Messianic Jews are passionate Zionists who embrace the current
nation state of Israel as God's chosen vehicle for the working out
of His salvation purposes in the world. Messianic Jews are unanimous in their view that Israel consists of ethnic Jews who have been

preserved by God through history to fulfill their destiny in the land of Israel.

By using a "plain sense" hermeneutic, the Messianic Jews view Israel's restoration (return and reestablishment) as indisputable. Their theological focus on the land of Israel indicates an assumption that Israel's restoration is firmly connected to the physical land of Israel and is an integral part of Israel's restoration. Israel as the Jewish people, as a nation in her ancient land has and yet will survive. Their reading of scripture sees God Himself as having ordained Israel to remain intact until the end of history. In the understanding of the Messianic Jew there is no dichotomy between physical and spiritual survival. Ethnic Israel is the embodiment of God's purposes for the world.

While Messianic Jews appreciate the universal nature of the Gospel and Yeshua's work of atonement, they hold the particularity of Israel (meaning the Jewish people) to be God ordained in perpetuity. Messianic Jews see no necessity to choose either the universal at the expense of the particular or to choose the particular over the universal. They can both be held in tension. Israel has been restored as a sign of God's faithfulness, even as evidence of God's existence and character. For the Messianic Jew, Israel **is** the visible witness to the world of God's purposes.

Endnotes

1   Katanacho, Yohanna, Christ is the Owner of the Land, (unpublished paper, Deerfield, Illinois, 2003),15.

2   Cohn-Sherbok, Dan, 'Introduction', in Dan Cohn-Sherbok (ed.), Voices of Messianic Judaism: Confronting Critical Issues Facing a Maturing Movement, (Baltimore, MA: Lederer, 2001), xi.

3   Messianic Jewish Alliance of America, Statement of Faith, www.mjaa. org/engine.cfm?i=2&sl=13, accessed 2/11/2006.

4   Shulam, Joseph, The Middle East Peace, Teaching from Zion – the Middle East Peace Talks – Oslo, 2003, www.Netivyah.org.il/ English%20Web/TFZ/ME%PeaceTalk.htm, accessed 2/11/2006.

5   Stern, D., 2000, "The Land from a Messianic Jewish Perspective," in *The Bible and the Land- an Encounter* Loden, Walker, Wood (ed.) , (Jerusalem: Musahala 2000), 42.

6   Nerel, G. (ed.), "Messianic Jews and the Modern Zionist Movement," in *Israel and Yeshua*, (Jerusalem: Caspari Center Elgvin, 1993), 75.

7   Evans, C. A., *Noncanonical Writings and New Testament Interpretation*, (Peabody: Hendrickson, 1992), 116.

8   Boskey, A. "The Messianic Use of Rabbinic Literature," Mishkan 8&9, Jerusalem, 1988, 25-74.

9   Juster, D., Biblical Authority, in *Voices of Messianic Judaism*, ed. Cohn-Sherbok (Baltimore, Maryland: Lederer, 2001), 25.

10 Kinzer, M. (2001), Scripture and Tradition, in *Voices of Messianic Judaism*, ed. Cohn-Sherbok, (Baltimore, Maryland: Lederer, 2001), 29.

11 Kinzer, M. Post-missionary Messianic Judaism, (Grand Rapids, Michigan: Brazos, 2005), 90.

12 Kinzer (2005), 105 .

13 Miller, D. "Messianic Judaism and the Theology of the Land," in Mishkan 26, Jerusalem, 1997, 31.

14 See for example, Urbach, C. "The Land of Israel in Scripture," in Mishkan 26, Jerusalem, 1997, 21-30.

15 Stern.

16 Fruchtenbaum, A. Israelogy: The Missing Link in Systematic Theology, (Dallas: Ariel, 1993); Hebrew Christianity - Its Theology, History and Philosophy, (Grand Rapids: Baker, 1974).

17 Skjott, B. "Messianic Believers and the Land of Israel - Survey," in Mishkan 26/1, Jerusalem, 1997, 75. This survey is of interest as it covers issues of the beliefs and attitudes of Messianic Jews living in Israel towards the land of Israel, Zionism, political affiliations, and relationships with Palestinian believers.

18 Skjott, 76.

19 Stern, 54.

20 Kivun, No.21, Nov./Dec. 2000, p.9. The respondent quoted is not a Messianic leader but is a member of a local Israeli Messianic congregation.

21 ibid. p.9.

5

Their Theology, Our Nightmare

MUBARAK AWAD

Psychiatrist

Greetings in the name of our Lord Jesus Christ who came to Palestine, lived under occupation and became an activist to help mankind to restore justice and to be a teacher for all of us to be humble, and to open our mind and hearts especially to those who are in need. I am a Christian Palestinian who was born in Jerusalem and who traces my Christian roots to the time of the original Disciples of Christ. I belong to the Orthodox Church (the Greek Orthodox Church). I completed my high school education at St. Georges School in Jerusalem. Both Palestine and I are the product of The Al Nakbah, the 1948 war, that we call "The Great Catastrophe". I am happy to be here to discuss the life of the Christian Palestinians. It is my hope that I can shed at least a little understanding of our situation and make known our existence in the Middle East in general and in the Holy Land in particular. I am a Palestinian activist who has participated in many negotiations with Israel for peace. I am a nonviolent pacifist who started the nonviolent movement in Palestine to resist Israeli military occupation. I stand here to tell you my story so that you will be more aware of the biblical theology of one group that has come about as a factor of many changes and suffering in the name of God. Some of you will be hearing from a Christian Palestinian for the first time. Perhaps some of you will question every word I say. My experience and the life I live are mine. I can't go back and change anything that has happened in my life. I am neither here to fit into any agenda, nor am I here to ask for your sympathy. I am here to give the facts of my life and experience so that you cannot say: "We have never heard the Palestinian Christian story". My hope is that after you hear the truth, as I know it, you will follow your inner spirit to preach justice, reconciliation and love for all mankind without prejudice and discrimination.

On a pleasant Sunday afternoon in July 2000 members and pastors belonging to local Palestinian evangelical congregations from the Palestinian territories gathered at the Bethlehem Hotel to celebrate the formation of their council. My brother Alex Awad (who is a Methodist minister in Jerusalem) related this event to me. An American woman, who was present at the meeting, approached one of the pastors and asked him if she could say a few words to the assembly. The pastor desiring to show courtesy to the guest asked the MC (also a Palestinian pastor) if the lady could say her few words. The MC, unaware of what was coming, agreed to let her talk. When the lady took the microphone, no one could believe the words that came out of her mouth. She professed to the Palestinian evangelical Christians assembled there that she had a word from the Lord for them. "God," she said, "wants you all to leave Israel and go to other Arab countries." She added that they must leave to make room for God's chosen people, the Jews. She warned the pastors and the audience that if they did not listen to the instructions, which God had given her, God would pour his wrath on them. When her agenda was recognized, one of the pastors came and whisked her away from the pulpit, but not before she served the whole assembly a mouthful of what is known today as Christian Zionism.

This is not an isolated example by an overzealous Christian Zionist; every one of those Palestinians pastors gathered in that assembly could tell similar stories. When I am invited to speak on behalf of the Palestinian cause in any church, seminary, University, or public group setting, there is always an attempt to have a balance to the presentation. The sponsoring group will invite a Jewish speaker, or an Israeli to counter what I have to say. This is true even if it is a Christian Arab gathering like Sabeel. The need to have a Jewish voice becomes a must, yet this same attempt at balance is not a requirement when a Jewish speaker speaks. There is no similar attempt to have a Palestinian voice in a point/counter point role. On one occasion I was with an Israeli official on a live TV debate on the Arab-Israeli conflict. When the time came for questions from the public, a man, after learning that I was a Palestinian Christian, called to tell me that if I was truly a Bible-believing Christian and a true follower of Jesus, I would know that God had given the Holy Land to the Jews and that I and other Palestinians Christians should peacefully leave the country. I am certain that most Christian Zionists are not as radical and confrontational as the woman and the man in my examples. However, many Christians in the United States and around the world cling to these ideas without critically examining them.

Influential TV evangelists in the United States, such as Pat Robertson and Jerry Falwell, both staunch advocates of Christian Zionism, have warned and threatened U.S. presidents against carrying out policies that would pressure Israel into making concessions to Palestinians on the pathway to concluding a peace agreement. They and other influential Christian Zionists have cautioned and manipulated presidents against forcing Israel to abandon Jewish settlements in the West Bank as part of a 'land for peace' deal.

1. What are the theological and eschatological (end time) beliefs of Christian Zionism?

- Jews have special favor with God and neither time, history nor the religious conditions of Jews can affect or alter God's special favor towards the Jewish people.

- The Holy Land belongs to the Jews. It always has and it always will. Neither history, nor the passing of centuries, nor the religious or moral condition of Jews today can alter this fact.

- Jews today are an extension of the Israelites in Biblical times. Therefore, just as the nations during the Old Testament era were judged as to how they treated ancient Israel, the same is true today. God will bless nations and individuals who bless the modern Jewish state and God will curse countries and individuals who curse it.

58

- Old Testament prophecies, although uttered thousands of years ago, are being fulfilled in Israel today and have been since 1948 when the state was born.

- God's 'end time' plan is directly connected with modern Israel. Christians can speed up the coming of Christ, as they help bring about the fulfillment of prophecies that are relevant to Israel.

2. Dangers of the Teachings of Christian Zionism

Most adherents of Christian Zionism are not aware of the destructive theological, religious and political implications of these ideas to us Palestinian Christians. These ideas threaten the continuous presence of Christians in the Holy Land and create tension between Jews and Christians, and division between evangelical Christians and main stream churches as well as between Moslems and the Christian minority.

3. Implications

To even say there are theological implications of Christian Zionism creates a contradiction in terms. Zionism is a secular political movement that has clear political goals and has been nonreligious from its conception. Because of the political positions of Zionism, millions of people around the world equate it with racism. Therefore it is not to the advantage of Christianity to be in union with Zionism. Zionism deviates from the heart of the New Testament. New Testament Christianity proclaims "For God so loved the world ...", while Christian Zionism proclaims 'for God so loved modern Israel'. According to the book of Acts, Jesus made clear to Peter in a vision that God no longer favors one nation over others:

> Then Peter began to speak: "I now realize how true it is that God does not show favoritism but accepts men from every nation who fear him and do what is right" (Acts 10:34-35).

In the epistle to the Galatians, St. Paul confronted a group in the churches of Asia Minor that wanted to drag the new believers back to Judaism. Paul stood firmly against this group teaching the churches that in Christ there is no Jew or Gentile but that both have equal access to God through Christ.

> You are all sons of God through faith in Christ Jesus, for all of you who were baptized into Christ have clothed yourselves with Christ. There is neither Jew nor Greek, slave nor free, male nor female, for you are all one in Christ Jesus. If you belong to Christ, then you are Abraham's seed, and heirs according to the promise (Gal 3:26-29)

Christian Zionism influences its followers to be indifferent to the Biblical mandates on peace and justice. Hard-line Christian Zionists teach that peace between Israel and her neighbors could only be established by the anti-Christ, the archenemy of Christ. Consequently, religious or political leaders or organizations that endeavor to make peace between Israelis and Palestinians can be seen as tools of the anti-Christ. Thus the more turmoil and suffering that the nations of the Middle East undergo the greater evidence that God is carrying out his eschatological program. Eschatology for many Christian Zionists is far more important than Biblical teachings on peace and justice. Jesus told some religious teachers who denied the importance of justice:

> Woe to you, teachers of the law and Pharisees, you hypocrites! You give a tenth of your spices — mint, dill and cummin. But you have neglected the more important matters of the law — justice, mercy and faithfulness. You should have practiced the latter, without neglecting the former (Matt. 23:23).

4. Religious Implications

Christian Zionism is adding fuel to the tension between Christians and Muslims. Many Christian Zionists, especially after 9/11, began to see Muslims as enemies of God. TV evangelists went on air publicly denouncing Muslims and Islam. Christian Zionists continue to talk about reaching the world for Christ. How can they do so when they are alienating and building walls of mistrust between them and over a billion Muslims? I have many Christian friends who became so angry about this "Christian" message that they have been hearing and the support these ideas give to Israel that they changed their religion to Islam. Many Arab Christians in Africa and especially in Egypt are converting to Islam. My Christian faith is creating an obstacle for me to live in my birthplace of Palestine. I am one of those who want to become a Jew so that I may have equal rights in my own country, but not because I feel Judaism is a better religion for me. The failure of the Christian leadership and this Christian obsession with the future vision of the Holy Land, propaganda that sides with Israel completely, denies my rights as a Christian. (By the way, no Rabbi will do the honor of letting me convert. They have received letters urging that I not be accepted as a Jew.)

Palestinian Christians have existed in the Holy Land since the day of Pentecost and have kept the torch of Christianity burning faithfully for the past two thousand years. If the Christian Zionist agenda is carried out, it will mean the death of Christianity in the Holy Land. The erosion of Christianity in her birthplace would be a loss for the body of Christ everywhere. Can we imagine the Holy Land devoid of the Christian presence and a church which has been a faithful witness for Christ since the day the church was born?

Zionism is militarizing the church. The influence of Zionism on U.S. Christians has helped alter the perceptions of Christians toward the Arab-Israeli conflict and the war in Iraq. Christian Zionists overwhelmingly supported the war in Iraq and continue to support oppressive Israeli measures in the West Bank. For example, the slaughter of tens of thousands of Iraqi men, women and children in Iraq goes unnoticed and unprotested because of their belief that George W. Bush is a dedicated Christian president who is carrying out the will of God. Likewise, Israel's disproportionate use of force against Palestinian civilians in refugee camps in Gaza and the West Bank is usually accepted by Christian Zionists. If condemned at all, it is equal to a slap on the wrist, while a disproportionate amount of blame is placed on the Palestinians who are, in every aspect of their lives, under Israeli control.

Unlike the prophets of the Old Testament, Christian Zionists have no prophetic words of rebuke for the state of Israel when the Jewish state indulges in oppression. Christian Zionists do not call for the state of Israel to do justice. Israel confiscates Palestinian land, demolishes the homes of the poor, destroys their agricultural land and siphons off their water resources, while many Christian Zionists continue to bless Israel and sing her praises. There are Israelis today, however, like the brave prophets of ancient Israel who do not hesitate to call their compatriots to pursue justice. Jeremiah reflected that courage when he said:

> ...O house of David, this is what the LORD says: 'Administer justice every morning; Rescue from the hand of his oppressor the one who has been robbed, or my wrath will break out and burn like fire because of the evil you have done — burn with no one to quench it' (Jer. 21:12).

In the Sermon on the Mount, Christ calls all his followers to be peacemakers (Matthew 5:9). His teachings are often referred to as *The Good News.* They are God's good news for the entire human race. Can we intentionally proclaim his teachings as good news for some but bad news for others? When the Bible is used to endorse the theft of countries and the suppression of nations, then the good news becomes bad news and the Bible is twisted into a manual for occupation.

There are several major problems with Christian Zionist positions from a theological point of view which I am sure will be discussed in this conference. I will mention a few here: its treatment of the Old Testament and skipping the entire New Testament, its vision of God as a tribal God interested only in the Hebrew tribe rather than a universal God who cares for all mankind, its ignoring of God's requirements of justice and obedience as conditions for God's blessing and success, its emphasis on militarism and power rather than spirituality and nonviolence and love of enemies, its taking biblical quotations out of context and clumsy attempts to apply them to modern historical events, its reliance on Old Testament concepts that have been specifically overturned by Jesus, its marginalizing of the role of the Church as God's people, its overemphasis on predictive aspects (which have been proven false again and again) rather than a prophetic message of speaking truth to the powerful.

But what I want to talk about today is the lack of compassion and human sensitivity associated with the positions of Christian Zionists for the real people living in the Holy Land, whether Jewish, Moslem or Christian Palestinians, all of whom are children of God, whom God loves and whom God sent his son to die for.

In this respect, I would like to quote from Mark 3:5 and point out to you, in particular, the attitude of Jesus. In this passage Jesus was angered and saddened at the hardness of heart of the Pharisees. These men were very interested in the theological question of whether it was strictly proper for Christ to heal on the Sabbath. They had no compassion or care for this child of Abraham whose arm was paralyzed and in need of healing.

It is my hope, that in debating the questions of Christian Zionism and Christian positions towards the Israeli-Palestinian question, you will not ignore the human element and the reality of suffering and show some compassion. I hope you will not continue to anger our Lord. This insensitivity is shown in the following areas:

The conflict: The Middle East is torn by conflict between Palestinians and Israelis. Rather than pray and work for peace and reconciliation, Christian Zionism seems almost gladly to proclaim the enmity between these two people to be eternal and irresolvable. In addition, Christian Zionism proclaims this enmity to be part of God's plan and work in history. It further calls on Christians to take sides with one party, claiming that that is God's side, and that Christians should support that side militarily, politically and financially, should be glad for its victories, and happy at the losses of the other party. Within Christian Zionism there seems to be no role for Christians as peacemakers. To the contrary, Christian Zionists have publicly criticized Israeli officials for compromising, and have urged them to take a hard line, and refuse any peace plan if it includes, as it must, compromises over land.

For Jews: Christian Zionism is eager and anxious for the end of times, and Armageddon, and the "good news" it proclaims for Jews is that this ushers in the destruction of all the Jews, except for 144,000 souls who will be converted to Christianity. Why do

Jewish intellectuals and Rabbis accept these premises and do not fight these distortions as discrimination against them, I do not understand. It seems to me that being killed or converted is not a good bet for their future. Why do they continue to play a religious and political game that threatens their own existence?

For Palestinians, there is no role or interest, in this Christian Zionist stance other than to see Palestinians as an obstacle to the fulfillment of end-day prophecy. At best, it is hoped they will act as the lightning rod to attract worldwide anger and the invasion of Israel by other countries (Russia, or the King of the North, or all the nations of the world,) who will attack Israel, starting Armageddon, in a major fight with massive slaughter. There is no room or appreciation for the Palestinians as a people, or for their rights in Palestine. They are dispensable! It is true in the Old Testament; the people living in the land of Canaan were destroyed "because of their sins". What are the sins of the Palestinian people to justify removing them and ethnically cleansing them to make room for the fulfillment of prophecy? To say that this is God's plan is to show the same insensitivity and hardness of heart that angered Christ in Mark 3:5. Does God need human help for the promotion of the end of time? God did not ask for help for the first coming of Jesus. Are these Christian Zionists becoming an obstacle to God's actual plan?

For Palestinian Christians, there is nothing but denial and lack of sympathy. In our suffering and difficulty, what does Christian Zionism say to us? It advises that we must vacate our homes and land and voluntarily leave them to new Jewish immigrants, simply pack up and leave. Must we betray our people, neighbors, our identity and language, our churches and institutions, and support Zionism to help bring about the Second Coming?

For justice, it is irrelevant. In the Old Testament, God required justice from his people, and repentance, and God punished their sins with defeat, and exile. In the End Times, according to Christian Zionism, that is irrelevant. What is important is God's plan for history, and whether Jews accept Christ, or even obey the teachings of Yahweh does not matter. God's plan for Jews and for history remains the same, and it is the duty of Christians to support Jews, regardless of their sinful behavior, or lack of justice, or whether their policies are good, bad, godly or sinful, virtuous or oppressive. The message is: "He who blesses Israel is blessed, and he who touches you touches the apple of God's eye." God is no longer the God of Justice, but the God of the Jews. He no longer requires obedience and repentance, but only blind loyalty and support for his pet, his spoiled, and his chosen tribe.

This message of indifference to justice and morality and to the suffering of Palestinians is not only projected at Israel, but also at the entire Moslem and Arab worlds. The reaction then is, "What kind of God do Christians believe in?" Is it any wonder that the Moslem world is angry at the U.S. and evangelical Christians for their Middle East policy?

The situation today is that Palestinians have had to pay the price of the creation of the state of Israel (Al Nakbah). The "ingathering of the Jews" created their dispossession and oppression. Thousands of Palestinians became refugees to make way for the creation of the State of Israel. Christian Zionism has no sympathy for their displacement and suffering. Some lost their homes, and those who remained became unwanted citizens in Israel. Almost 3 million Palestinians live under Israeli rule in occupied territories, with their land constantly taken for Jewish settlements, their human rights systematically violated. Their resistance to such occupation invites massive repressive measures. Their economy is under siege, and their children are starving, but, like the man with the paralyzed hand in Luke, this is of no concern to the modern Pharisees, whose hearts are hardened to such suffering. All they care about is biblical prophecy fulfillment according to their own interpretation.

There are massive violations of human rights in the Occupied Territories which violate international law, principles of justice, and common decency. Christian Zionists seem to have no interest in any of this, but view the "prophecy fulfillment" as justifying all of these violations, and as being, in any case, irrelevant to God's working out of his plan in history. That supposed "divine plan" trumps international law, human rights and concepts of decency.

Humanity, with considerable involvement of Christian values, has rejected racism and discrimination. Apartheid and all forms of racial discrimination are condemned everywhere, and some Christians even call it a sin to discriminate. Yet the State of Israel is built on the principle of discrimination, by Jews against non-Jews, including the indigenous population (Palestinian Christians and Moslems). Discrimination is systematic in Israel and justified on the basis that this is a Jewish state. Christian Zionists entirely exempt the state of Israel from obeying laws against racism and discrimination. They readily support the most tribal and discriminatory view of Jews as a chosen people who are, by virtue of divine dispensation, permitted and even required to discriminate against all others, including Christians, in Israel. Similarly, they seem to exempt them from all rules, of the requirements of justice, of international law, and even the possession of nuclear and weapons of mass destruction (WMD). Laws that favor Jews at the expense of Christians and Moslems in all areas of life, from residency, social benefits, housing, education, services, and jobs, which are not tolerated by Christians anywhere in the world, are accepted in Israel as an expression of God's actions and favor to Jews, and God's plan for the End Times.

Violence: Christ taught us to love our enemies, and taught us the way of peace and nonviolence. Yet Israel is a highly militarized state that lives by the sword, and is proud of its weapons industry, modern air force, technological sophistication of weapons, not to mention WMD and nuclear weapons. Christian Zionists share in this pride and proclaim the victories of Israel's armies to be signs of divine support and miracles of modern times, similar to Joshua's victories.

In my mind, it is clear that the interpretations of Christian Zionists run contrary to the Holy Scriptures, but the most important thing is that they run contrary to the message of Christ, of love, and caring for the poor, the sick, the weak and the powerless. Christ wants us to be his hands and feet, ministering to 'the least of these my brethren'. Christians are not to be like the scribes and Pharisees, with no love or care for human beings, but only for the letter of the law, and the keeping of the Sabbath.

If I were a Jew or a Gypsy, the Holocaust would be the most horrible event in history. If I were a black African, slavery and apartheid would stand out as most horrible. If I were a Native American, it would be the discovery of the new world and the white settlements which nearly ended my race. If I were an Armenian it would be the Ottoman and Turkish massacres. If I were Japanese, my horror would be the atom bomb and U.S.A.'s treatment of my race in the Second World War. If I were a resident of Nanjing, China, the worst hour for me would be the rape of Nanjing by the armed forces of Japan when between 200,000 and 300,000 thousand people were killed in one day, Dec. 13, 1937. If I were a Palestinian, it will be the Nakba, the 1948 war, that created Israel. If I were in Sudan it would be Darfur. I can go and on ... about humans killing each other without any mercy.

No one people, race or religion has a monopoly on human suffering, and it is not advisable to establish a hierarchy of suffering. There is only one humankind, not different kinds of races, some more privileged and some needing to make space for these in compensation for their suffering. This is even more true when believers in Jesus/Yeshua discuss issues of Christian Zionism and the conflict in the Middle East. Christ's teachings on love and justice, forgiveness and discernment against government politics take prevalence before twisted interpretation of Scripture and national loyalty.

6

The Political Reality of Living in Israel, with a Suggested Path towards Reconciliation

DAVID FRIEDMAN

Since most of you do not know me, I want to share a little about myself. This may also help you to understand my background and my interest in the subjects that are being discussed here over the next few days. I am a retired professor of Jewish Studies. My career has been in post-secondary education in Israel for the past 23 years. The subjects I normally taught included the History of Modern Israel and the History of the Holocaust.

I am the son of a human rights attorney. My father worked in Germany for 8 years after WWII in the prosecution of Nazi war criminals. He ended up being the chief of that division in the state of Baden-Wurttemberg, where I was born. To quote the American ideals, I was raised by my parents to cherish life, liberty and the pursuit of happiness. As a Jew, I was raised with the ideology of Rabbi Abraham Joshua Heschel, who was known for his participation in civil rights initiatives in the U.S. for African Americans.

Later, my father was the only Jewish president of the National Association for the Advancement of Colored People in our state of whom I am aware. He was also an attorney for the Anishinabe Native American tribe. One of the greatest honors in my life was when I was given the status of honorary chief by the Inupiat Native American tribe. My grandmother was both the first Jewish and first female candidate for public office in her state, in 1921. So, respect for the human rights of African Americans, Native Americans, women and Nazi war victims was something that I grew up with. I recall my parents hosting Holocaust survivors in our home from time to time, counseling them and being a shoulder on which they could cry. I well remember some of those painful cries, because hearing them made a strong impression on me as a child.

I filed a human rights abuse claim with the ACLU at age 15. Growing up, I suffered discrimination for being Jewish. That has continued on into my adulthood, when in recent years neo-Nazi activists and PLO (Palestinian Liberation Organization) sympathizers have threatened my life and those of my family members as recently as last year. All of this goes to say that I know about ethnic discrimination and hatred first hand.

In spite of the current and past enmity between my people and the Arab peoples, I made it a point, starting at age 22, to learn Arabic, Arab history, culture and literature. I earned a Master's Degree in Arabic, having studied under Fuad Ajami, Caesar Farah, Anwar Chejne, George Khoury and Assad Busool. I am the only Jewish person to hold a graduate degree in Arabic from this institution. I love people of Arab descent and accept Muslims as my equals before God. All this goes to say that the fate of the Arab people has concerned me from an early age.

Since the Communist era, I have been involved in successful reconciliation between Polish believers, German believers and Israeli Messianic Jews. As you can imagine, there were many issues, past sins and a painful history to work through in those initiatives. When I served as a synagogue rabbi, I wrote a letter on behalf of our congregation to the students and faculty at a Native American college. We expressed sympathy and support for their people and their societal struggles. That letter apologized, as well, for the attitudes that caused great pain for them in history. Thus, I believe in reconciliation and in making amends for the past, and then progressing toward normal relations for the present and future. And I believe with perfect faith that some day, Egyptians, Syrians, Iraqis and Israelis will all serve the One God and His Messiah together (cf. Isaiah 19:25). So I stand here today with confidence in God, that someday He will sort out and heal the peoples of the world. The question facing all of us, though, is what to do till that day comes.

With that hope, I have come here to speak about what it is like living in Israel today. I want you to see the world from my eyes. I am here today, as well, with suggestions as to how to progress on the path of reconciliation. I will say some difficult things for many of you to hear. These things may challenge your theological under-pinnings, and present a view of the Israeli-Arab conflict that you do not often hear publicized. When I speak today about the wrongs that people have committed, I am not personally attacking any individual. So please do not take my words in that way. I will try to be as irenic as I can be.

Let me open by stating that this conference is not merely looking at a two way problem. If this conference is going to take steps in encouraging reconciliation, there are more issues to consider than just the conflict between Israelis and Palestinians. There is a larger situation that has helped cause the crisis on my nation's borders. We have what I would term an historic three-way situation that concerns the Jewish world, the Christian church and the Arab people. All three of these entities are represented here, and all three entities have had a relationship with each other for centuries. We are enmeshed together in history and current world affairs. Anything that is done toward reconciliation should concern all three of us.

This past week at a Jewish-Arab reconciliation conference, I heard talks by Dr. Willem Ouwneel, a prominent Dutch Reformed theologian, and Pastor Steven Meester, his Dutch colleague. They both spoke out about the wrongs committed by the historic church that have caused and contributed to much of the current conflict in the Middle East.

Number one in Meester's estimation is *replacement theology* (i.e., replacing Israel in the promises of the Bible with the Christian church). This interpretation of scripture has spawned both theological and political anti-Semitism. This has resulted too often in history with Jews being killed in the name of Jesus. In addition, Ouwneel pointed out another travesty when he stated: *"It is impossible to imagine the current Islamic mindset without the last century of*

Christian European colonialism." Based upon his and Meester's presentations at the conference, there was a corresponding call to the European Christians present to renounce these wrongs committed against the Muslim world as well. These are namely *the advent of the Crusades and colonialism.*

As Ouwneel and Meester have brought out, there cannot be any meaningful Christian initiative toward reconciliation with the Jewish and Arab world if the Church does not renounce its own historic wrongs. I think that both Ouwneel and Meester made valid points. On a personal note, I think that before any Church entity sits in judgment of or is critical of Israel, such an entity needs to check its own part in contributing to Jewish suffering. I as a Jew ask: How can the Church stand in judgment of the Jewish and Israeli people if it hasn't dealt with its own checkered past towards us? My people have had to fight to the death for our very existence *without* the help of the Church, and too often that fight was against confessing members *of* the Church. Unfortunately, history shows us that the Church does not stand on any high moral ground by which to tell Israelis how to act. I am sorry if this offends some of you, but history speaks for itself, and I will be honest with you at this forum. Overall Church compliance during the Crusades, the Inquisition and Eastern European pogroms are the eyes through which Jewish people see the Church today. Realistically speaking, how could it be any different?

My grandmother grew up in Tsarist Russia. Her town was attacked each year by Russian Christians who burned down the synagogue. The local Russian orthodox priest always led this pogrom. Is it any wonder that she thought I was insane for believing in Yeshua as the Messiah? "How can you believe in him, when his followers burned down our synagogues?" was her question to me. Today, Jewish people will not listen to a Church that either spouts or participates in anti-Israeli action or rhetoric. I know that there is still work for the Church to complete in undoing the damage caused by the Holocaust before Jewish people will listen to Christians. Rabbi Arthur Waskow has written that "the Holocaust left Jewish people to struggle to trust (again), to connect, to make peace and to repair our sense of 'G-d in hiding.'" I agree with him. When my father's army unit liberated the Landsberger Death Camp in Germany, my father helped photograph the corpses of murdered Jews for the U.S. Army archives. He never forgave G-d for what he saw. In his shoes, could you? To me, this is a foremost example of what Rabbi Waskow means by "God in hiding." I grew up with God hiding.

Rabbi Waskow meant that due to the near extinction of European Jewish communities, our entire people have been left to fend for themselves to survive. In that experience, it is nigh to impossible to trust other people and to find God. Many Jewish people ask, 'where was God when Europe allowed a million Jewish children to be murdered?' Others heard the loud silence of the Catholic, Lutheran and Orthodox churches across Europe during Hitler's genocide. While the Church was claiming to be the representatives of Yeshua, on the whole it said little to nothing to save its local Jewish populations. One result of the Holocaust was to distance our people from our God. For the nation of Israel to be able to reconcile with both the Christian world and at least Arab Christians, the unfathomable damage that happened to us by complicity during the Holocaust must continue to be undone. There still remains unfinished work. If the Church represents the hands of the Jewish Messiah, then help us today. Help smooth our path to return to our God; help us be free to live our lives in our land, undisturbed by Muslim threats; help us forgive you by using your voice to give us a chance to live. You can do this by using your voice to affirm our existence as the Jewish state. You were silent 65 years ago when we needed you. Please don't be silent today; affirm our existence, work on obtaining our forgiveness. If you do this, I believe some good things can happen. I am here telling you today that only if this is done, will Israel ever listen to the voice of the Church.

So I believe that any Church entity that criticizes the Jewish state in the name of Jesus, given the history between the Church and the synagogue, is detrimental to my people ever seeing Messiah for who He is. If the Church engages in anti-Israeli action, Jesus is further driven away from his own people, compounding the historic sin of Christianity against Jewish civilization. I recommend the works of three Christian writers, Rev. Franklin Littell, Father Edward Flannery and practicing Catholic James Carroll, for further light on this subject. A famous rabbi once taught, *"Take the large piece of wood out of your own eye before you complain about the speck of sawdust in my eye."* Unless that's done, not much will be done in Jewish-Arab reconciliation. So my suggestion here today is that any reconciliation or statements issued from this group begin with the Christian clergy reaching out to Israelis, as well as to Arabs.

Now, I would like to share my suggestions for how to make a reconciliation effort between Messianic Jews and Christian Arabs that will have some influence. There is an approach to reconciliation that I have experienced that gives me hope for bringing a small dose of *tikkun olam* to the world. *Tikkun olam* is Hebrew for the concept in Judaism of *bringing a measure of healing and restoration to our broken world.* Last week, I participated in the steering committee meeting of a reconciliation effort. For lack of a better name, let me call it the Dutch Initiative of 2006. There were 30 of us on the steering committee, consisting of 4 Messianic Jews (3 of whom are Israelis), 12 Dutch and 14 Arab believers. The Arab believers were from Morocco, Tunisia, Israel, the Palestinian Authority areas, Egypt, Holland, Germany and France. We have been meeting for the past 3 years, praying with each other, hearing each other's hearts, and studying the scriptures together. We studied about the Land of Israel, the Jewish people, the covenants to Abraham, Isaac and Jacob, and the role of Arab peoples in the last era of human history.

Below I present the first conclusions of last week's Dutch Initiative 2006. These were unanimously agreed upon by all 30 members of the committee.

1. That God's covenant promises to Abraham were passed on to Isaac and then to Jacob,

2. That this covenant from God is bound to the people of Israel, who are bound by it eternally to the Land of Israel.

3. The Church needs to repent and apologize to the Jewish and Muslim worlds; to the Jewish world for the Crusades and Inquisition, as well as theologically based anti-Semitism. All these have

helped fuel the murder of an estimated 7 million Jewish people in the past 200 years alone; and apologize to the Muslim world, for the Crusades and for supporting colonialism, which helped birth the popular hate-filled, political expression of Islam that we see spreading across the globe today.

Additionally, the Arab believers present issued a unanimous and courageous statement as part of the Dutch Initiative 2006. I laud them for this step in reconciliation. I am quoting it in full for you:

In the beginning of Islam, our ancestors destroyed synagogues. The Jews were driven out of their houses by our ancestors; also in recent times, Jewish people had to flee due to the actions of our co-nationals. Jews were buried alive, Jewish families were scattered and throughout the ages we have been responsible for what is done to Jews. Our heart hurts when we see the chosen son of God, Israel, walking through the ages, miserable, despised, avoided, exiled and in pain, like the suffering servant of God in Isaiah 53. Looking at them, we are reminded of You, our Lord and Savior. Thousands of Jews have been murdered in Arab countries, sometimes directly by Muslim hands. Influenced by anti-Semitism and Islam, (Arab) Christians sometimes don't want to even say the name 'Jews'. From the earliest times, we have taken an arrogant and critical attitude to the Jews. We have not followed Your word in this (cf. Romans 11:18, 20). Lord, we acknowledge that our hands are bloodstained. Although Your word says of Jews that 'they are beloved for the fathers' sake (Romans 11:28), love is not characteristic of the attitude of Arab nations toward our Jewish brothers. Lord, we acknowledge our lack of love and our spiritual arrogance. We are even guilty of stealing the birthright of Israel. We, the Arabs, have replaced and destroyed Israel, saying that we ourselves are Israel, and that the covenant exclusively belongs to us. Although we cannot undo ages of evil, may we now find, in the spirit of real repentance, new ways to express our love to Israel. We pray for the protection of our Jewish brothers against calamities from their enemies. In all their tribulations, may they turn to You, their Rock and their Saviour. Where once we and our ancestors held Your chosen people in low esteem, we now want to love them and see them with Your eyes of love (cf. Deuteronomy 7:6 & Zephania 3:17). O Most High, give us now, we pray, the proper attitude to our Jewish brothers and sisters. Lord God, bind our hearts together with the hearts of Your chosen people Israel, because we together wait for the return of Jesus the Messiah.

We Messianic Jews who were there received these statements, and forgave our Arab brothers for any part in their people's long-standing hostile attitudes towards us. It was a precious, emotional and healing moment. The Arab affirmation of the scriptures that teach about God's enduring call to the Jewish people had special meaning. We Messianic Jews also *asked our Arab colleagues* for forgiveness for any unfit attitudes on our behalf. The action was two-way.

This, in my opinion, is the truest reconciliation thrust that I have ever seen between Jews and Arabs. The humility, the honesty and the acceptance of all people there was astounding.

In addition, led by Pastor Meester, the Dutch Christians publicly renounced their anti-Semitism with a like statement to the one I just read to you. The Dutch Christians there renounced any connection to the Crusades, apologizing to **both** Jewish and Arab attendees. The Jewish and Arab attendees freely forgave the Dutch Christians. For me, the past 3 years of working with these people is a sincere path to reconciliation. I also find that these Arab believers do not threaten nor denounce my country. Instead, as per their statement, they support and pray for us. The Arab believers there have come alongside us Israelis in the hope that we, Israel, will fulfill the great call to be God's nation of priests from Exodus 19:5-6 and Deuteronomy 4:5-8. I truly laud them and thank them. Their support of Israel's existence has made it easier for me to work alongside them.

May I then suggest that a beginning step for any Jewish-Arab reconciliation follow along the lines of this very successful pattern from the Dutch Initiative 2006. I certainly hope that the points of this initiative will be discussed at this conference.

I want to again stress the fact that during this conference, we can think of what should be. We can deliberate on what we'd like the Palestinian Authority and Israel to do, and we can criticize. But this won't be of any help at all. I will keep bringing us back to this point:

changes will occur only if Israel is clearly accepted as the independent Jewish state by the Muslim world. All change is dependent upon this foundational change. I don't want to throw the proverbial monkey wrench into the works, but I am not optimistic that this can ever happen. So we can have conference after conference, and make declaration upon declaration, and they will have zero effect on the actual situation. So again I say: my Baptist friends, if you want to help affect a positive political change in the Middle East, first repent toward the Israeli and Arab peoples. Then issue a strong challenge to the Muslim nations to accept Israel as an equal nation. I think this is the best step that you can take. What is happening in Lebanon, Gaza and Iraq will continue to happen. This is because the region is at war and war will continue until Israel is accepted. War is the express wish of Iran, Syria, Hamas and Hezbollah. Those four entities are having their way.

As the Church, you will not be effective to encourage any changes till these aforementioned steps happen. Even then, there are no guarantees. This isn't a pretty picture, but it's about time for the Church to see the hard, cold, cruel and vicious reality that the rejection of Israel causes in today's world. Our rejection has caused the Middle Eastern crisis for the past 50 plus years, and continues to do so. If Palestinians are serious about gaining a Western style of peace for their people, the best thing they can do is to convince the Palestinian Authority, Hezbollah and Syria to accept my nation. Boycotts, terror, and even non-violent protest will not bring Israel to collapse, for God has promised a future for the Jewish people in Israel. We are there to stay. A people who weathered the Holocaust and 58 years of continual warfare will go on. Believe it or not, if Israel and the Palestinians stood together for Israel's acceptance, it would lead to Palestinian independence. It's a horrid shame that on the 29th of November 1947, this direction wasn't taken by the Arab League. On that day, rejectionism ruled among the Arab nations, and does so until today.

Dismantling Jerusalem and dividing it up again, or simply taking it away from Israel, would constitute an unjust political act. It would definitely touch off another war. Jerusalem is the heart and soul of the Jewish world and *has been so for* 3,000 years. As recent as 1840, Jerusalem had a Jewish *majority population*. During 2,000 years of exile, our Diaspora communities prayed *6 times a day* for God to return us to the city that He had chosen for us (According to the Bible, Jerusalem **is** in the land inheritance of the tribe of Judah). A proposal to divide Jerusalem is akin to a suggestion to divide Mecca to allow non-Muslims to live there. How would Muslims feel about that? I find this proposal entirely unrealistic and, again, it would touch off a war.

I now wish to talk about the issue of peace. Let's first ask an honest question. It will help us see the day-to-day reality of life in the Middle East. *Who* possesses peace to give to Israel? What I mean is this...what entity exists that is able to guarantee survival to my nation and to my people in exchange for anything that we could do? The answer is: *no one.* The Palestinian Authority does not have peace to grant to us. Neither do the Palestinian people, because the PA rules over them, and speaks for them, and makes political decisions for them, whether they like it or not. That is the reality we in Israel face. The Oslo Accords were our gamble for peace, and they failed miserably. I put the blame squarely on Yassir Arafat and his ruling clique. At any rate, *it was a miserable failure.* Muslims who hate Israel and are committed to our destruction dominate the PA. Political peace with Israel is not in any of the stated plans of Ismail Haniyya, and is becoming a term seldom used by Mahmoud Abbas who, by the way, is wrongly portrayed as being a moderate. He has done 'peaceful' things like deny the Holocaust, which is a crime in many nations. He wrote, and I quote, "Zionists collaborated with the Nazis to murder Jews in a plot to gain sympathy for creation of the state of Israel." What an insult to 6 million Jewish victims, not to mention 3 million Polish and up to 20 million Russian victims of Hitler. Abbas is also believed to have provided the financing for the 1972 Munich Olympics Massacre. An Israeli civil rights group [on Israel's political *left*!] and a former PLO operative have both accused Abbas of arranging the financing of that horrendous murder spree. At this point, ruled by fundamentalist Hamas, the PA has no peace to give to Israel.

Another reality is that no matter with whom we could reconcile, there is always another entity that wants a piece of our land with no regard to our survival. Syria claims the Golan Heights, and our intelligence services tell us they have been preparing to go to war for it. Iran wants all of Israel annihilated, with no possibility of talking, no negotiations involved, nor are any possible. We are simply a target. With Syrian and Iranian help, Hezbollah is re-arming in its attempt to destroy Israel's northern towns. The PA, led by Hamas, wants all of modern Israel, which they continually announce is to be a fundamentalist Muslim, Hamas-controlled state. Operatives from the Islamic Jihad, Hamas, DFLP and the Al Aksa Martyrs Brigade are constantly attempting terror intrusions into our cities. Those who want to murder us besiege us. That is our reality. None of these entities has enough peace to give to Israel. This is what we in Israel have to work with, this is our daily reality. We have *no* peace partners.

On the larger scale, the Muslim world will always refuse to be at peace with Israel. In Europe and in the Western world, peace means that we sign treaties to end armed struggle. It means that we follow up with the normalization of relations. This peace between Israel and the Muslim world is unreachable, as Europeans and the Americas define it. This is because the European concept of peace is unknown in Muslim thought. Muslims have difficulty conceiving of reaching such a state with the *dar al-harb* (the non-Muslim world). In fact, it was a Jordanian professor of mine who emphasized that there is no equivalent word in Muslim thought for 'peace'. *Salam* is the Arabic word most often translated as "peace" in the English-speaking world. But this is inaccurate. *Salam* holds another concept in Muslim thought. *Salam* is the state of affairs that occurs in Islamic society when Muslims control the government, and society is run according to Islamic jurisprudence. This is *salam*, a conceptual state where Christians and Jews are considered *dhimmi*, or politically and socially subjugated groups. The Israeli author Bat Ye'or has written much about how Jewish communities were treated as a subjugated *dhimmi* population. I recommend her works for an understanding of this concept. American author and civil rights attorney Justus Weiner has written how Palestinian Christians suffer in PA areas due to Muslim discrimination. His research does not blame Israel.

Another concept that all of you need to become familiar with is that of *waqf*. This states that once a land area has been under Islamic rule, that it is the duty of Muslims to ensure the land area will always remain a Muslim domain. *Jihad* is the struggle to ensure that such lands remain under Muslim control. Israel was under Muslim control. The concept that the modern state of Israel is nothing but a Muslim *waqf* is reiterated by Hamas in its charter. It is on-line and you can read it there. This accepted concept in Islamic political thought means that Israel's existence will never be accepted by the Muslim political tide in the Middle East, including in the PA areas. This directly affects the ability of Dr. Awad and Dr. Saad's proposals to occur, for who is going to change the concept of *dhimmi*, or *waqf, salam* or *jihad?* The political outworking of these concepts is the dominant motivation in Middle Eastern political affairs. The last concept I'd like to familiarize you with is *hudna*. Yassir Arafat publicly stated in South Africa that when he signed the Oslo Accords, it was an act of *hudna. Hudna* is Arabic for a temporary cease-fire. The armistice ending Israel's War of Independence was a *hudna*. This means that when Israel signs a treaty with any Muslim dominated entity, it can only be a temporary agreement, until the Muslim entity decides that it is to their advantage to change policy. Look at the history of Israel's borders, and it will become clear that all peace agreements are considered *hudna*, temporary cease-fires until it is time to fight Israel again.

My point is this: the Muslim world cannot grant Israel the peace that you and I are looking for, because the very concept of a state of peace in Western terms, does not exist in Muslim thought. And let's again face reality. Some 95% of the Middle East is Muslim, and is working one way or another to cause the downfall of my country. The great majority of Muslim 'ulama' (clerics) do not adhere to the tolerant interpretation of the Qur'an of Sheikh Palazzi of Italy, or Sarah Nasr of Canada. The Non-Violence International Center's bibliography on Islam and Peace looks impressive, but these authors are not considered majority voices in Muslim jurisprudence today. Israel is directly and daily threatened by both pronouncements and military developments in Iran. Iran has only one reason to develop nuclear power plants—to destroy my country. The fascist genocidal tyrant Mahmoud Ahmadinejad is at least an honest despot. He says what he means. This anti-Semitic head of state said one year ago that Israel needed to be, and I quote, *"wiped off the face of the map."* As we sit here, Syria and Iran openly and defiantly continue to arm Hezbollah in Lebanon. Why? There is only one purpose—to destroy my country.

We are in an actual state of war. War brings a lot of things with it: problems, violence and bad attitudes. War is hell, and I agree that it is wrong, but that *is* Israel's reality. This is the state of affairs in which we live. This state of affairs is due to the refusal to accept us as a state. I would even argue that we haven't been accepted as a viable people group by the Muslim world since the 7th century. One need only read about Muhammad's expulsion of two Medinan Jewish tribes and the killing of all males over 12 in a third Jewish tribe to see the start of this attitude. Throughout Muslim history, *dhimmi* status, whatever way you cut it, is the eyes through which Jewish people have been officially perceived. As long as we are threatened, we will act like a threatened people. We will justifiably care first and foremost about the Jewish state surviving. A people bent on this very legitimate need *cannot* be expected by anyone to act altruistically. If you expect Israel to make peace with the PA, understand that the Muslim's world hatred and unwillingness to accept us must change or it simply won't happen. Sadly enough, this is exactly the scenario that we see being played out on the stage of the Middle East today. Sad to say, that is the true reality of life in Israel.

My Moroccan friend Muhammad, a former student in training to be an *imam*, told me that Israel is not at war against Hezbollah; Israel is at war against one billion Muslim people worldwide. These are *his* words, not mine. Since the 1950s, we have suffered an economic boycott by the Arab-nations. These 22 nations ascribe to the ideals of *jihad, hudna, salam* and *waqf*. We are not hated because we war in Gaza against Hamas. That could be solved. We are hated because we are a *dhimmi* people ruling in a conceptual *waqf* area. This is simply an affront to the Islamic ideal. These are the very words used by Hamas in their rhetoric.

Unfortunately, all goodwill aside, no Christian Arab entity has any peace to give to my country. We do not have enough land to give in exchange for promises of a fleeting peace. Last summer was a test case. We dismantled our towns in the Gaza Strip and withdrew. Immediately, synagogues were desecrated and Kassam rocket attacks against Israel began from Gaza. Today Gaza is illegally arming itself in quantities that are simply frightening. There is no peace partner to talk to on our southern & western borders. There is no peace partner to talk to on our northern border. We found that out this past summer. Christian Arabs cannot and certainly will not confront any Muslim political authorities to convince them that Israel must survive. Well-meaning people like Dr. Awad may say this at times, and anyone can say so to *you,* because you are a safe audience. All of us here would like to see peace in Israel and the PA areas. But the question is, peace on whose terms? I have yet to hear a proposed framework for a conceptual Western style of peace.

If I were a Palestinian, I would have been really angry at the PA, because in 2000-2001 at Camp David and Taba, Prime Minister Barak was willing to give Arafat 95% of what Arafat was demanding—95% of land and political demands. Arafat refused. He did not want peace on any terms. In fact, I would be really angry at the entire Palestinian leadership, who were offered a homeland in 1937, 1947 and 2000-2001, and each time have rejected the offer in lieu of first destroying the Jewish presence. I think it remarkable that Palestinians were offered anything after WWII, considering the fact that the leadership unabashedly supported the Nazis under Haj Amin El Husseini.

A major factor in my analyses is the fact that there have never been a people in the history of mankind as persecuted as my people. Palestinian people have no monopoly on persecution. If one wants to find out what it means to suffer genocide, ask my people. We lost 6 million people, including over 1 million children, just 60 years ago. In the past 100 years, 7 million Jews have been killed, some in the name of Christ (namely Tsarist Russian pogroms), some in the name of Aryanism (namely Hitler) and some in the name of fundamentalist Islam. The world did little to care for these Jewish victims. Though often the PLO's demagogues equate Israel with the Nazis in their anti-Semitic rhetoric, let us look at reality: is Israel like the Nazis? How many Palestinians have been killed by Israelis? 1 million? No. Half a million? No. A quarter of a million? No. 100,000? No. My point is this: the Jewish people know suffering from experience as well if not better than any people on earth. We also know when we *cannot* make ourselves more vulnerable, because the threat of us perishing has *always* been too close to us to ignore. For the past 2,000 years, this has been and *still is* the reality of being Jewish.

7

Palestinian Christian Responses to Conflict[1]

YOHANNA KATANACHO

Summary

There is real diversity amongst contemporary Palestinian Protestant theologians and their different responses to the state of Israel. This essay, as presented by Katanacho, groups four main categories of theology and responses to Israel: biographies, apologies, Liberation theology, and Reconciliation theologies.

In the category called **"biographies"**, he focuses on Baptist Evangelist Anis Shorresh, the late Anglican pastor Audeh Rantisi from Ramallah, and Lutheran Pastor Mitri Raheb from Bethlehem. As they tell their stories, the common thread is "a description of the dehumanizing Israeli injustices against a Palestinian Christian family."[2] The author shows how following Jesus Christ led to forgiveness, but also a call for justice, with a commitment to non-violence. Katanacho, after giving a brief statement that encapsulates each story, provides a helpful critique of their weaknesses.

A second category is **"apologies"**, and the contemporary Palestinian apologists whose work he summarizes are Anis Shorresh and Dr. Imad Shehadeh, President of the Jordan Evangelical Theological Seminary. Their apologies are more focused on the encounter with Islam, and deal primarily with the issues of the Trinity/Doctrine of God, Christology, and the nature of Scripture. Katanacho points out that, while they focus primarily on Islam in the writings mentioned, "they pave the way for addressing the Arab-Israeli conflict in light of Islamic doctrines." They and some other evangelical Arab writers embrace a dispensationalist approach to eschatology.

"Palestinian Liberation theology" is the third category for Katanacho, best represented by Dr. Naim Ateek, founder of *Sabeel*, the Palestinian Center for Liberation Theology in Jerusalem. Ateek strongly opposes Zionism and Christian Zionism, and Katanacho carefully summarizes the way in which Ateek's christological herme- neutic of the Old Testament is crucial. He shows how Ateek strug- gles with the issues of violence and holy war in the Old Testament, and biblical understandings of prophecy, the land, and justice. The other representative of this category is Dr. Mitri Raheb, whose posi- tion is presented in summary. Both are wisely critiqued.

"Reconciliation theologies" is the fourth category, repre- sented at first by Anglican Bishop Abu El-Assal and by Lutheran Bishop Munib Younan. Katanacho concludes with an overview of *Musalaha,* a ministry of reconciliation between Palestinian Chris- tians and Messianic Jews, led by Dr. Salim Munayer. Again, Kata- nacho gives a thoughtful evaluation of each position with critique.

Katanacho concludes his essay with a call to dialogue between Palestinian Christian theologians and writers, and also encourages dialogue with Islam, with Israeli Jews, and with Western Christians, showing how each dialogue may prove mutually beneficial, though the past has heavily burdened each relationship.

Endnotes

1 This article in its full length appears in ***Missiology***, so we are only able to give a brief summary. The paper was read in full at the confer- ence at IBTS in Prague on 14 November 2006.

2 p. 2.

Literature list from the original article

Abdel Haleem, M. A.. *The Qur'an*. Oxford: Oxford University, 2004.

Abu El-Assal, Riah. *Caught in Between: The Story of an Arab Palestinian Christian Israeli*. London: SPCK, 1999.

Andrew, Brother, and Al Janssen. *Light Force: A Stirring Account of the Church Caught in the Middle East Crossfire*. Grand Rapids: Revell, 2004.

Arthur, Bryson. *The Hermeneutics of the Cross: A Treatment and Development of Naim Ateek's Hermeneutical Key*. Faculty of Theology, Mar Elias Educational Institutions, 2002.

Ateek, Naim Stifan. *Justice and Only Justice: A Palestinian Theology of Liberation*. Maryknoll: Orbis, 1989

Ateek, Naim Stifan, Cedar Duaybis, and Maurine Tobin, eds.. *Challenging Christian Zionism: Theology, Politics and the Israel-Palestine Conflict*. London: Melisende, 2005.

Awad, Alex. *Through the Eyes of the Victims: The Story of the Arab-Israeli Conflict*. Bethlehem: Bethlehem Bible College, 2001.

Awad, Bishara. "Speaking from the Heart: The Palestinians and the Land of Their Fathers." In *The Bible and the Land*. L. Loden, P. Walker, and M. Wood, eds.. Jerusalem: Musalaha, 2000, 177-185.

Chacour, Elias, and David Hazard. *Blood Brothers*. Grand Rapids: Chosen Books, ²2003.

Chacour, Elias, and Mary E. Jensen. *We Belong to the Land: The Story of a Palestinian Israeli Who Lives for Peace and Reconciliation*. Notre Dame: University of Notre Dame, 2001.

Cragg, Kenneth. *The Arab Christian: A History in the Middle East*. Louisville: John Knox, 1991.

Freedman, H., and Maurice Simon, eds.. *Genesis I*. 3rd ed., Midrash Rabbah. London: Soncino, 1983.

Gervers, Michael, and Ramzi Jibran Bikhazi, eds.. *Conversion and Continuity: Indigenous Christian Communities in Islamic Lands, Eighth to Eighteenth Centuries*. Toronto: Pontifical Institute of Mediaeval Studies, 1990.

Goble, Phillip E., and Salim Munayer. *New Creation Book for Muslims*. Pasadena: Mandate, 1989

Griffith, Sidney Harrison. *Arabic Christianity in the Monasteries of Ninth-Century Palestine*. Burlington: Ashgate, 1992.

—. *The Beginnings of Christian Theology in Arabic: Muslim-Christian Encounters in the Early Islamic Period*. Burlington: Ashgate, 2002.

Hefley, James C., and Marti Hefley. *The Liberated Palestinian: The Anis Shorrosh Story*. Wheaton: Victor, 1975.

Horner, Norman A. *A Guide to Christian Churches in the Middle East: Present-Day Christianity in the Middle East and North Africa*. Elkhart: Mission Focus, 1989.

Jarjour, Riad. "The Future of Christians in the Arab World." in *Who Are the Christians in the Middle East?* B. J. Bailey and J. M. Bailey, eds.. Grand Rapids: Eerdmans, 2003, 12-21.

Katanacho, Yohanna. "Christ is the Owner of Haaretz." *Christian Scholar's Review* 34(4). 2005, 425-441.

Kincaid, Jack and Ron Brackin. *Between Two Fires: The Untold Story of Palestinian Christians*. Gainesville: Banner Communications, 2002.

Maalouf, Tony. *Arabs in the Shadow of Israel: The Unfolding of God's Prophetic Plan for Ishmael's Line*. Grand Rapids: Kregel, 2003.

Mansour, Atallah. *Narrow Gate Churches: The Christian Presence in the Holy Land Under Muslim and Jewish Rule*. Pasadena: Hope, 2004.

Massad, Hanna. *The Theological Foundation for Reconciliation between the Palestinian Christians and the Messianic Jews."* Ph.D. dissertation, Fuller Theological Seminary, Pasadena, 2000.

Munayer, Salim. "Reconciliation and the Cross." Musalaha Reconciliation Ministries, 2006. www.musalaha.org/articles/CR.htm (Accessed January 16, 2006).

—. "Relations between Religions in Historic Palestine and the Future Prospects: Christians and Jews." in *Christians in the Holy Land*. M. Prior and W. Taylor, eds.. London: World of Islam Festival Trust, 1995, 143-150.

—. "Reconciliation from a Palestinian Point of View and the Challenge to the Jewish Believers." in *Seeking and Pursuing Peace: The Process, the Pain, and the Product*. Salim Munayer, ed.. Jerusalem: Musalaha, 1998a, 103-106.

—. "What is Peace?" in *Seeking and Pursuing Peace: The Process, the Pain, and the Product*. Salim Munayer, ed. Pp. 67-72. Jerusalem: Musalaha, 1998b.

—. *"The Ethnic Identity of Palestinian Arab Christian Adolescents in Israel."* Ph.D. dissertation, University of Wales, Oxford, 2000.

—. "On the Road to Reconciliation." *Mishkan* 35:32-40, 2001.

—. "Who Hates More? Who Is More Evil?" in *In the Footsteps of Our Father Abraham.* Salim Munayer, ed. Pp. 103-108. Jerusalem: Musalaha, 2002.

O'Mahony, Anthony. *Palestinian Christians: Religion, Politics, and Society in the Holy Land.* London: Melisende, 1999.

—. *The Christian Communities of Jerusalem and the Holy Land: Studies in History, Religion and Politics.* Cardiff: University of Wales, 2003.

O'Mahony, Anthony, Göran Gunner, and Kevork Hintlian. *The Christian Heritage in the Holy Land.* London: Scorpion Cavendish, 1995.

Odeh, Yousif. *Almajeea Althani Lilmassih [The Second Coming of Christ].* Kufr Yassif: Odeh, 2003.

Prior, Michael, and William Taylor, eds.. *Christians in the Holy Land.* London: World of Islam Festival Trust, 1994.

Raheb, Mitri. *I am a Palestinian Christian.* R. Gritsch, trans. Minneapolis: Fortress, 1995.

—. *Bethlehem Besieged: Stories of Hope in Times of Trouble.* Minneapolis: Fortress, 2004.

Rantisi, Audeh G., and Ralph K. Beebe. *Blessed are the Peacemakers: A Palestinian Christian in the Occupied West Bank.* Grand Rapids: Zondervan, 1990.

Register, Ray G. *Back to Jerusalem: Church Planting Movements in the Holy Land.* Enumclaw: WinePress, 2000.

Sabella, Bernard. "Religious and Ethnic Communities." in *Encyclopedia of the Palestinians.* Philip Mattar, ed.. New York: Facts on File, 2000, 346-349.

Sakhnini, Fouad. "The Gospel and Arab Thinking." in *Prophecy in the Making: Messages Prepared for Jerusalem Conference on Biblical Prophecy.* Carl Henry, ed. Carol Stream: Creation House, 1971.

Shehadeh, Imad N. *"Ishmael in Relation to the Promises of Abraham."* Th.M. thesis, Dallas Theological Seminary, 1986.

—. *"A Comparison and a Contrast between the Prologue of John's Gospel and Qur'anic Surah 5."* Th.D. dissertation, Dallas Theological Seminary, 1990.

—. "Additional Reasons for Islam's Rejection of Biblical Christology." *Bibliotheca Sacra* 161, 2004a, 398-412.

—. "Do Muslims and Christians Believe in the Same God?" *Bibliotheca sacra* 161, 2004b, 14-26.

—. "The Predicament of Islamic Monotheism." *Bibliotheca sacra* 161, 2004c, 142-162.

—. "Reasons for Islam's Rejection of Biblical Christology." *Bibliotheca sacra* 161, 2004d, 274-288.

Shorrosh, Anis. *Jesus, Prophecy & Middle East*. Daphne: Anis Shorrosh Evangelistic Association, 1979.

—. *Islam Revealed: A Christian Arab's View of Islam*. Nashville: T. Nelson, *1988*.

—. *The True Furqan*. Duncanville: World Wide Printing, ^{3}2002.

—. Islam: *A Threat or a Challenge*. Fairhope, AL: Nall, 2004.

Talal, Hassan bin. *Christianity in the Arab World*. London: Arabesque, 1995.

Trimingham, J. Spencer. *Christianity among the Arabs in Pre-Islamic Times*. New York: Seabury, 1979.

Wagner, Donald E. *Dying in the Land of Promise: Palestine and Palestinian Christianity from Pentecost to 2000*. London: Melisende, 2001.

Younan, Munib, and Frederick M. Strickert. *Witnessing for Peace: In Jerusalem and the World*. Minneapolis: Fortress, 2003.

A Biblical Theology of Israel and the Recent History of the Near East

RON DIPROSE

1. Introduction: Why the Recent History of the Near East cannot be understood without "a Biblical Theology of Israel"

Among the things I did in preparing for this conference was to read Norman G. Finkelstein's book Image and Reality of the Israel–Palestine Conflict.[1] While, in the dedicatory page, Finkelstein expresses the hope that he will never forget what was done to the Jews during the Shoah, he is very critical of the modus operandi of the Israeli State. In his opinion the only language Israel understands is force.

Finkelstein's analysis is purely secular. This is surprising considering the religious rhetoric used in the Arab world with reference to the Israeli-Palestinian conflict. By way of example, Article 13 of the Statute of the Hamas Islamic Resistance Movement states:

> Peace initiatives, and international conferences for resolving the Palestinian problem, contradict all the beliefs of the Islamic Resistance Movement. In reality, giving up any part of Palestine (including the territory that the UN assigned to Israel and that Hamas considers inalienable and not available to others), is tantamount to ceding part of the religion. The nationalism of the Islamic Resistance Movement is part of its religion and teaches its members to adhere to the reli-

gion and lift up the banner of Allah on their homeland while they engage in *Jihad*.[2]

According to this logic, events like the present Conference contradict "all the beliefs of the Islamic Resistance Movement". The Hamas Statute does not envisage reaching any agreement with the state of Israel, the existence of which it refuses to recognise; rather it envisages the *restitution to Allah* of all territory which the international community has assigned to Israel. The presumed Islamic rights to Israeli territory have motivated many similar calls in recent years for the extinction of the state of Israel.[3] One particularly vocal political leader who has recently expressed the wish that Israel be cancelled from the world map is the Iranian president, Mahmoud Ahmadinejad, who links Israel's demise with a more general eschatological vision of the return of the Twelfth Imam of Shi'ia Islam.[4]

Had Finkelstein taken into consideration the religious polemic of many who adamantly refuse to accept the existence of an enduring State of Israel,[5] he might have evaluated Israel's "language of force" somewhat differently. *Hudna* style diplomacy, which envisages a temporary truce, before a return to pursuing a stated policy of annihilation, cannot be expected to convince Israel to engage in serious dialogue. Speaking of peace has little meaning so long as one partner in dialogue retains a political/religious strategy which decrees the eventual annihilation of the other partner. What makes this threat even more ominous is Jewish awareness that their personal survival is closely tied to the survival of the Israeli State. A long history of being the butt of discrimination and violence, including the Russian pogroms and the *Shoah*, has produced the conviction, even in assimilated Jews like the Austrian Theodor Herzl, sent to Paris to cover the Alfred Dreyfus trial in 1895, that Jewish survival requires the existence of a Jewish State.

Another aspect of Israeli policy with which Finkelstein, and indeed many others, take issue, is the effort made to ensure that the majority of citizens of the democratic State of Israel be Jewish. On this point the government of Israel could be forgiven if she appealed to the very purpose of the Balfour Declaration, issued by the British government in 1917, which had in view "the establishment in Palestine of a national home for Jewish people" or to chapter 2, point 6, of the United Nations Resolution 181 (29 November, 1947) which envisaged only a minority presence of Arabs and Jews, respectively, in the Israeli and Palestinian States after partition.

More important, for the theme of this paper, is the seemingly intentional neglect, on the part of many, of the biblical vision of the unique relationship, decreed by God, between Israel and the land.[6] Insomuch as Christendom accepts the Hebrew Scriptures as part of its Holy Bible, a cavalier attitude towards their testimony to this relationship is out of place. The grounding of the unique relationship between Israel and the Land in divine promise, which has yet to find complete fulfilment (Ezekiel 47:15-20), may throw some light on the unusual circumstance of an international organ such as the United Nations decreeing the establishment of a Jewish State after a Diaspora of almost 2000 years, as well as the subsequent survival of this State, despite the refusal of most of its neighbours to recognise its existence.

It is increasingly common to read and hear the expression "Christian Zionism" being used in relation to the birth and survival of the modern State of Israel, as though the rebirth of the Jewish State were the fruit of a theological construct developed by Christians[7] while its survival depended on the support given by Zionist Christians.[8] Apart from the fact that the help given by Zionist Christians pales before that given by the American Jewish community, it needs to be remembered that the term "Zionism" is derived from the Hebrew Bible (Psalm 132:13-18 and *passim*). Moreover the development of the Zionist movement depended largely on events in Russia in the XIX century[9] and on the secular document *Der Judenstaat* written by Theodor Herzl in 1896.

More generally, the seed of the modern Zionist movement was already in the very soul of the Jewish people throughout their 2000 years of Diaspora. What else can account for the wish expressed annually at Passover: "next year in Jerusalem"? It is no accident that this wish has been linked with the Passover celebration. In other words it has been part and parcel of the religious hope of the people. There are other evidences that memory, religion and thoughts of the land are closely linked in Jewish culture. In his book *The Israelis,* Amos Elon gives some interesting examples of this. He relates how "Chaim Weizmann, the first President of Israel, was once asked by a British commission by what right the Jews claimed possession of Palestine. He is said to have answered: 'Memory is right'. Other nations too have occupied lands and then abandoned them. The point is that they did not remember, but the Jews never forgot Palestine". He also tells the personal story of the Polish Jew known to history as David Ben Gurion and those of Ukrainian Jewish Socialists who felt a compulsion to return to the Land and dedicate their lives to developing it.[10]

While modern Israel may seem to be a very secular state, it must be remembered that her claim to the land has strong religious roots. In this regard there is a significant difference, when compared with Arab references to religious roots, in the way these claims are grounded: the Hebrew Bible explicitly links Israel's national and religious identity with the land promised to Abraham, Isaac and Jacob. For example the city of Jerusalem, closely linked with the king David, the Davidic dynasty and the centralisation of the worship of YHWH (2 Sam. chs 5-7 and *passim*), is mentioned over 700 times in the Hebrew Bible but not once in the Koran. These writings also stress the permanency of the relationship between Abraham, Isaac, Jacob and their descendants with the promised land (Genesis 15:18; 17:8; 28:13-14; Psalm 105:7-11).[11] The evidence of these passages is often suppressed by interpreting them allegorically, together with all references to a future messianic kingdom centred in Jerusalem. This hermeneutical device is used to justify the substitution of Israel, as a subject, with the Church which is thought to have permanently replaced Israel as mediator of the Kingdom.[12]

The question is whether this is a legitimate way of interpreting the Hebrew Scriptures. Marvin Wilson states that it is rather a form of Neo-Marcionism (as the God of the OT was demoted by Marcion, just so Israel, the second protagonist and addressee of much in these writings, is demoted by the exponents of Replacement Theology).[13] When coming to a decision on this point the recent history of Israel surely needs to be taken into account. Few would deny that the Bible has an eschatological dimension. If this is true, it implies that not all predictive prophecy can be spiritualised away or applied to the present. Eschatological hope is often closely related to the future of the chosen people, the Promised Land and Jerusalem.

In view of these considerations it seems appropriate, in a discussion on the Israeli-Palestinian conflict, to outline a Biblical Theology of Israel before considering briefly what implications this theology has for understanding recent history in the Near East.

2. A Biblical Theology of Israel

Besides being important for understanding the underlying issues in the Israeli-Palestinian conflict, the development of a Biblical Theology of Israel is called for, for the simple reason that Israel features as the second great protagonist in the Bible, after God himself. This is demonstrated statistically by over 2000 mentions of Israel in the Hebrew Bible and 73 mentions in the New Testament writings. Thus, if Christian theology is justified in developing what is called Ecclesiology, Christian theologians are bound to recognise the need for a Theology of Israel, a subject even more strongly grounded in the Biblical story.

Because space is limited, I will build this introduction to a Biblical Theology of Israel around a specific theme, that of national election, with a brief mention of the covenants which God made with his chosen people.

2.1 The Fact of National Election

The Bible recognises the fact that before Israel existed there had already been a long history of nations and empires (Genesis chs 1-11). By way of illustration, there is evidence that the Sumerian people lived in a region to the north of the Persian Gulf around 4500 B.C., or 2500 years before the time of Abraham. Similarly the golden age of the Egyptian pyramids and of the relative literature dates back to the III millennium B.C., well before the existence of Israel.

The creation of an elect people who descended from Abraham, Isaac and Jacob is presented in the Scriptures as being part of a design to bring blessing to the entire world (Genesis 12:1-3 and *passim*). In order that this promised universal blessing could become a reality, it was necessary that the patriarchs and their descendants have a special relationship with God.

The Hebrew verb used to describe God's choice of Israel is *bakhar*. Moses affirmed the fact of national election in these terms: "Because... [YHWH] loved your forefathers and chose their descendants after them, he brought you out of Egypt by his Presence and his great strength" (Deuteronomy 4:37). And again: "For you are a people holy to the LORD your God. The LORD your God has chosen you out of all the peoples on the face of the earth to be his people, his treasured possession" (7:6). In the continuation of this passage Moses stresses the fact that God's decision to choose Israel was not based on any special merit, rather it was a free choice (vv. 7-8; cf. 14:1-2; 26:18-19). In a similar way God chose Jerusalem, the city of David, as "a dwelling for his Name", where his people were ordered to meet to offer sacrifices and for the main national festivals (16:6, 16-17; 26:1-2; 1 Kings 8:16-21; 11:34-36). In all of these passages the accent is put on God's free choice.

The Greek verb used to translate *bakhar* in the LXX is *eklegomai* (the middle voice of eklegô). *Eklegomai,* besides carrying the active meaning of "choose", retains something of the reflexive sense of "choose *for one-self*". This corresponds to what the Hebrew Scriptures teach concerning the Creator's relationship with Israel (Exodus 4:22-23) and Jerusalem (2 Chronicles 6:5-6), chosen for his own glory (Isaiah 43:1-7; 48:1-11; 62:1-12). The adjective *eklektos* ("elect" or "chosen one") describes the person or thing chosen, while the noun ekloge ("election") indicates the action of the one who chooses. The same terms are used in the literature of the New Covenant (see below).

Israel's special relationship with God was recognised by the Canaanite peoples before the nation entered the Promised Land (see Joshua 2:8-11). Rahab acknowledged to the spies sent by Joshua: "the Lord your God is god in heaven above and on the earth below" (v. 11), while Balaam described Israel as "a people who live apart and do not consider themselves one of the nations" (Numbers

23:9). He further defined them as a people whom God had brought out of Egypt (24:8), and he added: "May those who bless you be blessed, and those who curse you be cursed!" (24:9).

Almost a thousand years after the events of the Exodus, Haman used the following argument to persuade King Xerxes of Persia of the reasonableness of his project to have Israel destroyed: "there is a certain people dispersed and scattered among the peoples in all the provinces of your kingdom whose customs are different from those of all other people and who do not obey the king's laws; it is not in the king's best interest to tolerate them" (Esther 3:8).

2.2 The Nature of National Election

Israel's status as an elect nation is unique (Amos 3:2). However her election is linked with the realisation of divine purposes which go well beyond the personal interests of individual Israelites. In this sense the national election of Israel is similar to Jesus' action in "electing" some of his disciples as "apostles": "[Jesus] called his disciples to him and chose [Gk. *eklezamenos*, from eklegô] twelve of them, whom he also designated apostles" (Luke 6:13). National election does not guarantee the eternal salvation of all generations of Israelites who have lived from the time of the patriarchs, just as the election of the Twelve did not guarantee their eternal salvation, as the sad story of Judah Iscariot demonstrates (Luke 6:16; John 6:70-71; 17:12; Acts 1:15-25).

What national election does guarantee is that the purposes for which God created this nation will be realised (see below). It also guarantees the nation's survival in view of playing its part in the realisation of the purposes of her election (see Jeremiah 31:35-37; Isaiah 66:22). Moreover it guarantees that Israel would return to the land promised to Abraham and his descendants in the case of the nation having been exiled on account of her unfaithfulness (Leviticus 26:40-45). Finally it implies that the survivors of the nation will repent, experience salvation and enter the New Covenant when "the deliverer will come from Zion" to "turn godlessness away from Jacob" (Romans 11:25-27; cf. Isaiah 53:1-6; 59:20-21; Zachariah 12:10-14).

2.3 The Biblical Covenants

Before considering the *purposes* of Israel's election, a brief mention should be made of the Biblical covenants. The fact and nature of Israel's status as an elect nation is governed by the covenants into which God entered with this and with no other nation.[14]

The most important of these is the covenant which God made with Abraham, Isaac and Jacob.[15] The fundamental and enduring nature of this covenant is confirmed repeatedly throughout the Bible.[16] This covenant is both conditional (the right to enjoy its promises is based on obedience) and unconditional (fulfilment of its promises depends entirely on God). This is illustrated by the fact that the generation of Israelites who left Egypt died in the desert because of unbelief while Israel as a nation entered the Promised Land according to the terms of God's covenant with Abraham (cf. Deuteronomy 30:1-10).

The most spectacular covenant ceremony involving God and Israel was the one which took place in several steps at Mt Sinai (Exodus 19:1 – 24:18; 34:1-28). The apostle Paul sums up the relationship between the patriarchal covenant and the Sinai covenant with these words: "The law, introduced 430 years later, does not set aside the covenant previously established by God and thus do away with the promise. ... It was added because of transgressions until the Seed to whom the promise referred had come" (Galatians 3:17, 19).

Two more covenants are essential parts of a Biblical theology of Israel, the Davidic covenant[17] and the New covenant.[18] In the covenant God established with King David the concept of progeny was enriched by the following elements: kingship, a dynasty, a throne and a kingdom which would endure forever.

The New Covenant, while promised to Israel, was enlarged to include all who experience the blessing of salvation, because its operational basis is the unique, eternal sacrifice of Israel's Messiah (Luke 22:20; 24:45-47). At the same time the fact that the nation of Israel was the primary addressee in Jeremiah 31:31-34 was confirmed on the day of Pentecost when thousands of Israelites were the first to enter the New Covenant (Acts 2:14-41; cf. chs 3-6) and will be further confirmed when "all Israel" will be saved and will enter into its blessings (Romans 11:25-27).

We can now return to the main theme, national election, and consider briefly the purposes which govern God's special relationship with this people.

2.4 The purposes of Israel's Election

It is possible to distinguish between a general purpose (i) and specific purposes whereby the general purpose is realised (ii.– v.).

i. The general purpose for which God created and elected Israel can be stated simply: *God chose Israel primarily for himself, as a way of manifesting his glory within the context of human history* (Isaiah 43:1-7).

ii. Israel was to be *"a kingdom of priests and a holy nation"* (Exodus 19:5-6). Besides the priestly role of Aaron and his descendants, in the services of the tabernacle and the temple, the entire nation was to have a priestly role as standing between God and the other nations of the world.

iii. Israel was called *to receive, put into writing and preserve special revelation* (Deuteronomy 4:5-8, 6:6-9; cf. Romans 3:1-2). Special revelation is closely linked with the history of the elect nation. It follows that, in order to understand special revelation, we must give careful attention to the history of Israel. Although other peoples developed philosophies and religious traditions, they remained in the dark regarding the revelation of God's purposes for mankind, until they came into contact with the revelation entrusted to Israel.

iv. YHWII called the descendants of Jacob *to know and believe in him and to be his special witnesses* (Isaiah 43:1, 10-11). This role can be seen in the events recorded in Daniel chapters 1–6, where the false claims of the Babylonian religion and the inflexible witness of Daniel and his three Jewish friends to YHWH are the main themes (see in particular 2:47; 3:29; 4:34-37; cf. 1 Maccabees chs 1– 4).

v. God chose Israel *to be instrumental in bringing his blessing to "all peoples on earth"* (Genesis 12:3). In relation to this purpose Israel was to be instrumental in bringing the Messiah into the world (Romans 9:5) and through him the possibility of eternal salvation for all humanity (John 4:22; cf. Isaiah 49:5-6). Included in the purpose of bringing blessing to all peoples, is the future role of Israel in a kingdom of peace and righteousness associated with the second Advent of the Messiah (Genesis 49:10; Isaiah 11:1-11; 61:2b-9; Ezekiel 34:24-31; cf. Acts 3:21; Revelation 19:11–20:9).

A careful consideration of the first four purposes listed above will reveal that they parallel closely the purposes of the church, composed of Jews and Gentiles, which Christ is in the process of building (Matthew 16:18; Ephesians 2:11-22; 3:20-21; 1 Peter 2:1-10; Mark 16:15-16; Romans 10:14-18; 1 Thessalonians 1:6-10). However even now Israel's witness to God's presence in history retains a specificity to be distinguished from the witness of the Jewish/Gentile church to the gospel of grace.[19]

When it is remembered that the members of the church are described as members of the "body" of the Messiah (Ephesians 1:22-23) it appears logical that the purposes entrusted to the church should be similar to those previously entrusted exclusively to the chosen people. When noticing this parallelism of purposes, it is appropriate that the church recognise its debt to Israel.

The fifth purpose of Israel's election is closely linked with the institutional distinctions between Israel and the church. In order to accomplish God's design of bringing blessing to "all peoples on earth", Israel was given a political as well as a theocratic structure, and a territory with which the Name and honour of God would be forever associated (Psalm 105:4-11). Once Israel was introduced into the land of promise, she was obliged to organise her life, both socially and religiously, around a calendar of annual events, and according to the social and religious decrees, revealed to Moses on Mount Sinai.[20]

That all this implies roles for Israel never envisaged for the church, can be illustrated by the circumstance of Israel having to engage in war with God's enemies. This is alluded to in a word God spoke to Abraham while the Mosaic law provides specific legislation concerning how to do this. Passages such as Genesis 15:13-16 and Deuteronomy 20 legitimise the conquest of the land at the time of Joshua (see the book of Joshua), as well as the wars conducted by Saul and David against the Philistines (1-2 Samuel). The institutional distinctions between Israel and the church can also be seen in the fact that the Hebrew prophets make it clear that the land of Israel and the city of Jerusalem in particular, will be the locus of the future messianic kingdom (see Isaiah 2:1-4; 61:2-9; Ezekiel 37:21-28; Zachariah 8 and *passim*; cf. 1 Corinthians 15:25-28; and Satan's final attempt to oppose God by marshalling his forces around the "beloved city", Revelation 20:9).

2.5 National election in the New Testament

In the New Testament the question of national election is treated explicitly only in Romans 9 –11. Paul's main concern in these chapters is to define Israel's relationship with the gospel of grace. In this context the question of national election is basic, as is shown by Paul's summing up of his argument:

> As far as the gospel is concerned, they are enemies on your account; but as far as election is concerned, they are loved on account of the patriarchs, for God's gifts and his call are irrevocable. Just as you who were at one time disobedient to God have now received mercy as a result of their disobedience, so they too have now become disobedient in order that they too may now receive mercy as a result of God's mercy to you. For God has bound all men over to disobedience so that he may have mercy on them all (Romans 11:28-32).

The reference to national election is evidenced in the whole of this section of Romans by the sudden introduction of the term "Israel" at 9:6 and the repeated use of the term in all three chapters. In fact "Israel" is used eleven times in this section of Romans, not once elsewhere in the letter and only six times elsewhere in all of Paul's letters. This sudden change in nomenclature (cf. 1:16; 2:9-10, 14, 25-29; 3:20; 15:26) is accompanied by historical references concerning how God freely formed and chose his elect people (9:1-13). In this passage Paul uses the term "election" (Gk. *ekloge*) to qualify the descendants of Abraham, Isaac and Jacob (v. 11), drawing attention to the fact that the exceptional manner of the birth of Isaac confirms that the choice corresponded to "God's purpose". The fact that the same term is used in 11:28 with reference to all the descendants of Jacob, including the part of the nation which at present remains in a state of unbelief, demonstrates beyond all doubt that national election is not cancelled by the fact that the whole nation has not yet recognised Jesus as their Messiah and thus believed the gospel of grace.

The fact that the elect status of Israel remains, regardless of the failure of many individual Israelites to recognise Jesus as the Messiah (11:5-10), demonstrates the faithfulness of God and thus the certainty of the salvation accomplished by Christ and applied in the life of the believer by the Holy Spirit (Romans 8:1-39).

It might be helpful to summarise at this point what Romans 9–11 teaches concerning the election of ethnic Israel. 1. Election removes all doubt that God will accomplish what he has revealed to Israel (11:28-29); 2. It ensures that even her present "transgression" means riches for the Gentiles, because it favours the propagation of the message of salvation and thus reconciliation with God, and that the effect of the future re-admission of the "natural branches" at present broken off from the olive tree will be similar to bringing "life from the dead" (11:11-12, 15); 3. It does *not* entail election to salvation for those members of the nation who do not respond by faith in Christ, described by Paul as "the end of the law so that there may be righteousness for everyone who believes" (10:4), however it *does* imply the future salvation of "all Israel" (11:25-27); 4. Finally, it does *not* put limits on the administration of the mercy of God; on the contrary it ensures its universal scope (11:30-32).

2.6 Being God's chosen people is not always a bed of roses

The beginning of God's message to Israel through Amos is very instructive: "Hear this word the LORD has spoken against you, O people of Israel – against the whole family I brought up out of

Egypt: 'You only have I chosen of all the families of the earth; therefore I will punish you for all your sins' " (Amos 3:1-2). While another nation, which has not been given God's law, may experience reprieve at God's hand, the privileges experienced by Israel and her role as the special witness of YHWH, mean that she will be punished for all her sins.

Furthermore, an awareness of Israel's status as an elect people tends to exacerbate latent anti-Semitism. So from Haman's plot to exterminate Israel in the fifth century B.C., through to modern times, being a member of the elect nation often means suffering at the hands of the other non-chosen peoples. Tevye, the main character in the well-known musical and cinema production *Fiddler on the Roof,* who was forced to carve out a meagre existence in the village of Anatevka, in Tsarist Russia, amidst continual threats of pogroms, speaks for many Jews when he utters the following words to God: "I know we are a chosen people, but once in a while couldn't you choose someone else?".

3. Implications of our study for understanding recent history

The preservation of Israel and her partial return to the land promised to Abraham, Isaac and Jacob, should be seen as being primarily for the sake of God's name and because he is faithful to his covenant, not as something which Israel herself has merited (*cf.* Deuteronomy 9:4-6; 12:4-28; Leviticus 26:40-45).

The question often arises as to whether recognition of the modern State of Israel[21], as a step towards the fulfilment of God's plan for his elect people, implies approval of Israeli government policy and its outworking. An honest reading of the Biblical prophets would suggest rather that the believer should approve or criticise the decisions and activities of the Israeli government in the light of the Torah revealed at Mt. Sinai. On the one hand, the Torah teaches that Israel would inherit the land promised to Abraham, Isaac and Jacob and that, at times, she would need to engage in war against her enemies. In Numbers 10:9, YHWH commands: "When you go into battle in your own land against an enemy who is oppressing you, sound a blast of the trumpets. Then you will be remembered by the LORD your God and rescued from your enemies." On the other hand, the prophet Micah, echoing the requirements of the Torah, tells Israel "to act justly and to love mercy and to walk humbly with your God" (Micah 6:8). This implies many things, including the banning of moral perversity such as Gay Pride marches. It also requires that Israel return to "acknowledge the LORD" (Hosea 6:1-3).

We will now take the risky step of considering a chapter of recent history in the Near East, which involves Israel. In the year 2000 Israeli troops abandoned southern Lebanon in accordance with UN Resolution 425 and in August 2005 Israeli troops ensured that all Israeli citizens leave the territory of Gaza. In response the Hezbollah amassed missiles in southern Lebanon and began systematic attacks on northern Israel, while from Gaza terrorist attacks, backed by Hamas, have continued on southern Israel. During the summer of 2006 there have been incursions into Israeli territory from Gaza and Lebanon, the killing of some Israeli soldiers and taking captive of others, actions which were tantamount to a declaration of war. On July 12, 2006 Israel retaliated and for 34 days waged war, intentionally against the Hezbollah in southern Lebanon and Hamas positions in Gaza. All the while, the Hezbollah continued to launch missiles, some calculate the number at 4000, into northern Israel.

The result of the war has been mixed. The Israeli strategy for disarming the Hezbollah left thousands dead, many of whom were not Hezbollah. Meanwhile the Hezbollah leader, Nasrallah, claims that the Hezbollah have won the war and declares that they have no intention to complete the process of disarmament (envisaged by a UN resolution).

What should our reaction to Israel's retaliatory action be? On a practical level the choice is made easier by the example given by Israel itself. As a democracy Israel feels very free to criticise herself,[22] so why should *we* refrain from objective criticism? Of course this means bearing in mind the barrage of missiles fired from Gaza at peaceful settlements in southern Israel, and the tunnels constructed and used to kidnap Israeli soldiers, following Ariel Sharon's withdrawal in August 2005. Similarly we must take into consideration the existence of an infrastructure in southern Lebanon whose declared purpose is to barrage Israel in view of her destruction. We certainly should not follow the example of systematically condemning the retaliatory actions of the Israeli army while remaining silent when Palestinian suicide bombers seek the indiscriminate destruction of Israeli civilians.[23]

While exercising our right to criticise Israel's handling of a war, or any other aspect of her public life, we should not be blind to other factors, such as Israel's contribution to science and medicine, which is disproportionately great, compared to the size of the population. Neither should it cause us to forget what inspires much of the fervour of suicide bombers and others ready to sacrifice their lives in the torrent of hate directed against Israel.

The real issue is the right of Israel to exist as a Jewish state. Hamas denies this right and makes no secret of the fact that she is working to a strategy aimed at destroying Israel.[24] Our position on this question will be determined, in part, by the weight we attribute to the Biblical theology of Israel. If we say the church *is Israel* and that we are now living in all that history can ever expect to know of the messianic kingdom,[25] then we might consider Israel's presence in the Near East illegitimate, despite the fact that her claim is firmly grounded in the Hebrew Bible. If, on the other hand, we accept, with Paul, that "God did not reject his people, whom he foreknew", we will recognise Israel's right to dwell in the land, while at the same time caring for the plight of all men and praying and working for their salvation.

Endnotes

1   G. Finkelstein, *Image and Reality of the Israel–Palestine Conflict,* 2nd ed., London – New York, Verso, 2001.

2   See Carlo Panella, *Il libro nero dei regimi islamici,* Milano, Rizzoli, 2006, p. 403; cf. art. 22, where the PLO (Palestinian Liberation Organization) is criticised for adopting the ideology of a non religious state: "Lay ideology is diametrically opposed to religious thought" (ibid., p. 405).

3   Yasser Arafat, the former leader of the PLO, made no secret of his goal
     to conquer Jerusalem and the whole of Israel, linking this with the will
     of Allah (for example, in his speech on his 70th birthday, ICEJ News
     Service, August 6, 1999). Feisal Al-Husseini, his minister for Jeru-
     salem, said publicly in 1994: "For us peace means the destruction of
     Israel. We are preparing for the final war... we have become dangerous
     enemies of Israel. We will not rest... until we have destroyed Israel"
     (*Bulletin of the Jerusalem Institute for Western Defence*, Bulletin 2,
     June 1994, quoted in www.ilvangelo.org/israelestart.htm).

4   The two speeches delivered by Ahmadinejad before the United Nations
     General Assembly, respectively on 17 Sept. 2005 and 20 Sept. 2006,
     enshrine both his description of Israel as an illegal occupier of Palestin-
     ian territory and his vision of preparing the world for the coming of the
     Twelfth Iman.

5   It must be recognised that a vocal Islamic minority does not share this
     view. For example Prof. Abdul Hadi Palazzi, Secretary General of the
     Italian Moslem Association, at the third International Seminar on The
     Sources of Contemporary Law, July, 1996, Jerusalem, affirmed that
     anti-Zionism cannot be found in Islamic classical sources but is the
     fruit of "the transformation of Islam from a religion into a secularized
     ideology". He continues: "This was originally done by the late Mufti
     of Jerusalem, Amin al-Husseini, who was responsible for most of the
     Arab defeats and during World War II collaborated with Adolf Hitler".
     He continued: "Both Koran and Torah indicate quite clearly that the
     link between the Children of Israel and the Land of Canaan does not
     depend on any kind of colonization project – but directly on the will of
     God Almighty. As we learn from Jewish and Islamic Scriptures, God,
     through His chosen servant Moses, decided to free the offspring of
     Jacob from slavery in Egypt and to make them the inheritors of the
     Promised Land. Whoever claims that Jewish sovereignty over Pales-
     tine is something recent and dependent on political machinations is
     in fact denying the history of revelation and prophecy, as well as the
     clear teaching of the Holy Books". He cites Sura 5:22-23 in support
     of this statement and adds: "the Holy Koran quite openly refers to the
     reinstatement of the Jews in the land before the Last Judgment, where
     it says: 'And thereafter We said to the Children of Israel: Dwell securely
     in the Promised Land. And when the last warning will come to pass,
     We will gather you together in a mingled crowd' " (Sura 17:104, "The
     Night Journey"). Moreover Sura 2:145, reads: "They would not follow
     thy direction of prayer (*qibla*) nor art thou to follow their direction of
     prayer; nor indeed will they follow each other's direction of prayer".
     Palazzi comments: "As opposed to what 'Islamic' fundamentalists con-
     tinuously claim, the Book of Islam – as we have just seen – recognizes
     Jerusalem as the Jewish direction of prayer". He concludes: "As no one
     wishes to deny Moslems complete sovereignty over Mecca, from an

Islamic point of view there is no sound theological reason to deny Jews the same right over Jerusalem". (Root and Branch Association, www. rb.org.il).

6   For example all contributors, except Rowan Williams, Archbishop of Canterbury, at the 5th International Sabeel Conference held at the Notre Dame Ecumenical Centre, Jerusalem, April 14-18, 2004, failed to give serious consideration to this aspect. Cf. note. 4 above.

7   This seemed to be the presupposition of many of the contributors at the 5th International Sabeel Conference, the theme of which was: "Challenging Christian Zionism: Theology, Politics and the Palestine-Israel Conflict".

8   For example the following statement can be read in an article on Zionism which appears on www.riforma.net.: "Without the continual political support of Zionist Christians in America, and significant economic help given by the United States government, it is very unlikely that the State of Israel would have survived after 1948 and would have continued to occupy the West Bank since 1967".

9   See Amos Elon, *The Israelis: Founders and Sons,* London, Sphere Books, 1972.

10 Ibid., pp. 25-26, 82-83.

11 Cf. W. D. Davies, *The Territorial Dimension of Judaism,* Berkeley, University of California Press, 1982. Davies observes that the Land is part of the essence of Judaism (ibid., p. 53).

12 For an in-depth examination into the question of the origin of Replacement Theology and its effects on Christian thought and practice, see my book: Ronald E. Diprose, *Israel and the Church,* Waynesboro, GA, Authentic Media, 2004; Italian ed. *Israele e la Chiesa,* Roma, IBEI Edizioni, 1998; German ed. *Israel aus der Sicht der Gemeinde,* edition Wiedenest, Hammerbrücke, jota-Publikationen, 2001; French ed. *Israël dans le développement de la pensée chrétienne,* Saone, France, La Joie de l'Éternel, 2004.

13 Marvin R. Wilson, *Our Father Abraham: Jewish Roots of the Christian Faith,* Grand Rapids, MI, Eerdmans, p. 110.

14 This finds strong confirmation in Romans 9:4 and Ephesians 2:11-12.

15 See Genesis 12:1-3, 7; 13:14-17; 15:1-21; 22:15-18; 26:3-4, 24; 28:13-15.

16 See, among others, the following passages: Exodus 2:23-25; 6:2-8; 32:11-14; Leviticus 26:40-42; 2 Kings 13:22-23; Galatians 3:15-18.

17 See 2 Samuel 7:11-16; 1 Chronicles 17:10b-15; Psalms 2, 89; 2 Samuel 23:1-5; Jeremiah 23:5-6; 33:14-16, 23-26; Ezekiel 37:24-25; Hosea 3:4-5; Amos 9:11; 1 Kings 11:13; Luke 1:68-75.

18 Jeremiah 31:31-34; cf. Isaiah 55:3; 59:21; 61:8-9; Ezekiel 16:60; 34:25-31; 37:26-28; Romans 11:25-27.

19 Cf. Matthew 24:32-34 where the best translation of the term *genea* is "race" or "people".

20 For a more complete treatment of the question of the institutional differences between Israel and the Church, see Gordon R. Lewis and Bruce A. Demarest, *Integrative Theology,* Three volumes in one, Grand Rapids, MI, Zondervan, 1996, 339-340.

21 Officially established as a sovereign state on May 14th, 1948, on the basis of the UN Resolution of November 29th 1947.

22 For example, on September 13, 2006 the Israeli Defense Minister, Amir Peretz publicly admitted that there had been failures during the war against Lebanese Hezbollah guerrillas. There have also been public demonstrations criticising the handling of the war, calling for a commission of enquiry into the three leaders who were responsible for leading it: the Defense Minister, the Prime Minister Ehud Olmert and the army chief of staff, Lieutenant General Dan Halutz, *International Herald Tribune,* Thursday, September 14, 2006, p. 5.

23 In a protest note, dated 28 August, 2006, the Prime Minister of Israel, Ehud Omert, observed that while "out of 175 United Nations Security Council resolutions up to 1990, 97 were against Israel; out of 690 General Assembly resolutions, 429 were against Israel", the UN remains strangely silent when Israel is attacked.

24 See articles 13 and 14 of the Hamas Statute; cf. the claim to Hezbollah's right to engage in armed resistance against Israel, made by the Hezbollah military commander, the Sheikh Nabil Qaouk, in the *Daily Star,* Beirut, 3 October, 2006.

25 See note 11.

9

How Shall We Interpret Scripture about the Land and Eschatology? Jewish and Arab Perspectives

PHILIP SAA'D

1. Introduction

There is no other conflict in the world which is similar to the Israeli-Palestinian conflict. For the last one hundred years the land of Israel/Palestine has witnessed a continuing struggle between the Jews and the Palestinian people. Several evil wars have erupted, tens of thousands have been killed, and hundred of thousands have been stripped of their lands and property and are even now displaced. Not only the Middle East, but the whole world is actually aflame as a result of this conflict between the Jews and the Arabs.

One might ask, what is the reason behind all this constant struggle and bloodshed? Supporters of Israel say, "It is the unwillingness of the militant groups, such as Hamas and Islamic Jihad to accept Israel's existence in the land of their ancestors." But, on the other side, the Palestinians, in particular, and the whole Arab and Islamic world, in general, insist that the real cause today is the continuing occupation of the West Bank and Gaza strip, the growing number of settlements in the Palestinian territories, and the severe oppression under which the Palestinians have been placed by the Israelis.

Perhaps each side has some legitimacy for their claims. However, we as a world wide Christian community and followers of Jesus

Christ, especially the Messianic Jewish community and Palestinian Christians in the Land, have a mandate, even a commission from God to do something in the midst of this terrible situation. We were not asked by the Lord to solve these problems, because we cannot. We have been commissioned by Him to proclaim the Gospel of Christ which can transform lives, and reconcile people with God and with each other. It is Jesus alone who can replace enmity with love and turn war into peace. It is very important for us as followers of Jesus to open our eyes and see that the source and the roots of this ancient conflict are not found in different political positions but in deep religious and theological convictions.

The three monotheistic religions were and still are involved in this conflict. The hostility and the violence, which have lasted almost one hundred years in the land of Israel/Palestine, were and still are motivated by religious convictions. The killing is being committed in the name of God. Each party claims the ownership of this little piece of land, and says that it is theirs as a gift from God. These claims are, of course, according to their beliefs and interpretations.

A similar theological and religious interpretation of land ownership and of the relationship with God was raised many centuries ago by a Samaritan woman, who had an encounter with a Jewish rabbi called Jesus. "Sir," the woman said, "I can see that you are a prophet. Our fathers worshiped on this mountain, but Jews claim that the place where we must worship is in Jerusalem." (John 4:19-20). The apostles of Jesus were also nationalistic, they had some kind of exclusive mentality toward the ownership of the land, right before Jesus' ascension, they asked him, 'So when they met together, they asked him, "Lord, are you at this time going to restore the kingdom to Israel?" This kind of Zionistic aspiration, which they had, was the same as that of the rest of the Jews of today. They based their claims on their understanding of God's scriptural promise given to Abraham and his descendants (Genesis 15:18-20).

The Jewish people claim that their right to the land is based on biblical promises. They believe that God promised the Land to Abraham and to his descendents 'the Jews' and that this promise of ownership is unconditional and eternal.

The Muslims have also similar claims; they ascribe their rights to the land of Palestine to religious and historical reasons. Hamas, the Palestinian Islamic Resistance Movement, in their covenant, article 11 declares, 'Palestine is Islamic *Waqf* till Judgment Day. No part of it should be given up' [1]. The second Palestinian uprising was called *'Intifadat-el-aqsa'*, with "el aqsa" alluding to the large, historic mosque in Jerusalem. They also claim the land for themselves; they base their claims on **their** religious convictions. They are ready to kill and also to be killed to achieve that purpose.

There is no doubt that the Crusaders invaded the land of Israel/ Palestine in the Middle Ages because of religious claims. Since then Christians in the Middle East, in general, and in Israel/Palestine, in particular, have suffered persecution and tension because of these so-called Christian holy wars. They are still being accused of being crusaders. Thousands of Christians have left the land as a result of this continuing religious tension. Theology of the land and eschatology are for the peoples of the Land matters of life and death.

This long struggle over the land and the divergent theological positions related to it, have unfortunately, exerted a tremendous impact on the followers of Jesus Christ in Israel/Palestine. These issues have caused disunity and lack of fellowship between the Messianic Jewish community and the Palestinian Christians. Although the two groups give allegiance to the same Lord, 'Jesus Christ', and consider the scriptures, Old and New Testaments, as their final source of authority in faith and practice; yet they are divided in their biblical interpretation and theological positions related to the Land and Eschatology. As a result of these divisions they are lukewarm in their fellowship with each other.

Let us look now at the divergent hermeneutical interpretations and the theological perspectives over these issues of land and eschatology. We have already heard some good and comprehensive descriptions of the Messianic views; therefore there is no need to elaborate in detail on this side of the coin.

2. Messianic Jewish perspective

It is difficult to be objective when it comes to hermeneutics. A personal hermeneutic is made up of the background, the affiliation, the nationality, the training, the life experience of a person. All of these things put together build up some kind of presuppositions and shape a person's hermeneutic. It is important to be aware of this fact from the beginning.

Messianic Jews draw their interpretation and their biblical perspective concerning the land, from their ethnic identity as Jews, and from their Western and evangelical background. Most of the pioneers of this modern day movement in Israel, and most of the adherents, came to the land from the West already as converted believers in Jesus of Nazareth as the Messiah. Some came as gentile Christians married to converted Jewish spouses, they came to the land already under Western theological influence. Most of these people came with a premillennial dispensational theology.

One survey, which was conducted about ten years ago, among a small number of Messianic Jews living in the land, showed that the vast majority of those surveyed understand that God promises the Land to the Jewish people, and that promise is eternal and unconditional.[2] Most of the Messianic Jews have a literal interpretive approach to the issues of the Land and Eschatology.

David Miller, who takes this kind of literal hermeneutic, in his article "Messianic Judaism and the Theology of the land" says:

> The history of the Jewish people begins with the call of Abraham... From that time the national and spiritual history of the Jewish people has been inseparably linked with the land of promise. Through out the ages, the Jewish people have believed that their presence in the land was a result of God's faithfulness to the covenant which he made with Abraham, and when they have been dispersed from the land they have been confident that this same faithfulness would some-day restore them. The covenant which God made with Abraham was unconditional, irrevocable and confirmed with an oath.[3]

Another Messianic Jewish author, Dr. David Stern, expresses a similar literal perspective. He says:

The promise of the Land of Israel is forever, and the plain sense of this is that the Jewish people will possess the land (at least in trusteeship) and live there. To say that this New Covenant transforms this plain sense into an assertion that those who believe in Yeshua come into some vague spiritual 'possession' or a spiritual 'territory' is intellectual slight of hand aiming at denying, canceling and reducing to naught a real promise given to a real people in the real world.[4]

Lisa Loden believes that Dr. Stern employs here a literal or 'plain sense' hermeneutic. It is an interesting approach in that he includes not only Israel and the Church as those to whom the land is relevant, but adds a third element the Messianic Jewish body of believers, who are fully part of both groups.[5]

Not all Messianic Jews have this literal premillenial dispensational approach. Baruch Maoz, the pastor of a large Messianic congregation in south Tel Aviv, prefers to call himself a Christian Jew rather than a Messianic Jew, he says, "I am a Christian and Zionist, but I am not a Christian-Zionist." Maoz appreciates Western evangelical support for the Jewish people but denies their motivation. He says, in addressing one of the most influential American dispensational leaders, Pastor Haggee, "The almost total lack of moral consideration represented by Mr. Haggee's professedly Christian support of Israel, is less than Christian." Pastor Baruch Maoz appreciates the encouragement of Mr. Haggee for his people, but he wishes it were more biblically informed. Maoz says that the true focus in the message of Israel's prophets was always spiritual and moral, the predictive element had last place and was always subservient to the former two. He says that Hagee's theology is a militant, crusader type of Christianity that seems to have missed the central themes of reconciliation, forgiveness, and non-violence that are at the heart of Jesus' message and ministry. Pastor Maoz acknowledges and understands the different cultures among the body of Christ in the land, that the relationships between the children of God, Jews and Arabs, are more important than one's nationality.

In conclusion, we notice that Christian Jews such as Rev. Maoz do not emphasize Land or Last days' theology, but evangelism, kingdom ethics and unity in the body of Christ. However, the vast majority of this community in Israel, take the promise of the land and the return to it as literal and eternal, the land belongs to the Jews alone, and that the secular state of Israel is a sign of a biblical prophecy fulfillment.

3. Palestinian perspectives

Most of the literature related to the theology of the land and eschatology in Israel/Palestine has been written by Messianic Jewish writers. Unfortunately little of that literature was written by Palestinian Christians. There are several reasons for this fact, some of those reasons were mentioned earlier. As mentioned, most of the Messianic Jews, who are active and talented in writing, came from western countries. They came to Israel well educated and trained in seminaries and universities. They came with a mission to reach their people for the Messiah and serve their new state the best way they could. Christian and Messianic organizations from abroad helped start study and publishing centers in the Land with the purpose of helping and supporting the growing Messianic community. After the Six Day War in 1967, which resulted in the occupation of the West Bank (Judea and Samaria), Gaza and the Golan Heights, thousands of religious Jews settled on the mountains of Judea and Samaria. Those settlers were motivated by a religious Jewish Zionism that interprets the promise of the land literally and unconditionally to the Jewish people. As a result of this, the Palestinian resistance was taken to a higher dimension. This new situation, the increasing number of settlements in the occupied territories and the escalation of the Palestinian resistance, made the issue of the land and Bible prophecy, once again very relevant. Messianic Jewish writers who usually interpret the Bible literally, started writing their theology on these issues with greater effort. Much of the Messianic theology was written and developed in this period of time. With this kind of theology, they served their people and their state in a powerful way. With the help of the dispensationalists in the West they contributed a great deal of worldwide support to Israel, the land and the people.

It was also after this Six Day War that the Palestinian Christians became involved in this great theological endeavor, they developed their own hermeneutic and started writing their own theology on the issues of the land and eschatology. Most of Christian Arab population was not yet theologically trained. Yet it is important to remember that the historical Christian churches in Palestine were always at the front in the Arab intellectual and political awakening in Israel/Palestine and in the rest of the Arab world. They were the first to write history, literature, poetry and political science. In some Arab countries they led their people toward independence, democracy and the struggle for human rights.

The situation which emerged after the Six Day War demanded from this Palestinian Christian community that they think and work for the survival of their people. Most of the Palestinian writings were political. The pioneers in this area were again nominal Christian Arabs. The Christian writings started to flow only after the first *intifada*. The Muslims were the ones who took part in and were involved with the political and physical struggle. Palestinian Christians who were always passive in relation to war and non-violence, did not take part in the Palestinian physical resistance against Israel. Yet out of obligation toward their people who were suffering, displaced and oppressed, the Christian Arab community started with, what I call, a theological *intifada*. They went back to their source of faith, to the Bible, they started using it to fight their theological battle against occupation, against the literal interpretation of the Bible and against the danger of Christian Zionism. They looked in the Bible for answers and for ways to defend their people against the state of Israel and against those who claim that the almighty God gave them the Land and it is theirs.

A new Palestinian theology of the Land was developed at this stage. The writings were for the purpose of supporting the Palestinian cause, and for dialogue with their Messianic Jewish brothers and sisters in the Land. They were hoping that together Palestinian Christians and Israeli Messianic Jews would form a united prophetic Christian body which could stand for justice and against state oppression. There was a great need also to confront the dangerous influence of the Christian Zionists and refute their theology, a theology which supports Israel unconditionally, ignores the basic humanitarian needs of the Palestinian people and endangers the very existence of the Palestinian Church in Palestine. In such a difficult situation as this the Christian community had to act, without compromising their faith in the Bible and out of an obligation to take part in their people's struggle for respect, and for a peaceful and secure life in the land.

Different streams of theology were developed among the Palestinian Christian community, such as liberation theology led by Dr. Naim Ateek, and a hermeneutic of the poor and the oppressed which was developed by Dr. Mitri Elraheb, a Lutheran pastor living in Bethlehem. Other streams of theology, developed in the Christian Arab sector, is the amillennialism, Replacement theology and the Covenant of Grace theology. Though these streams of theology are different in terms of hermeneutic, they have one thing in common, which unites all the adherents: it is their strong rejection of dispensationalism and of a literal interpretation of the Bible. It is interesting that there are a few Palestinian believers and church leaders who are not influenced by the political situation but still believe in premillennial, dispensational theology.

It is important to note that this theological 'uprising' was developed mainly in the West Bank, where the issues of the Land are very relevant. In recent years a phenomenon of palestinization has also occurred among the Christian Arabs who live in Israel. The conflict has influenced their thinking and understanding of the prophecies which are related to the Land and eschatology. Some have shifted from premillennial theology to amillennial. Others, mainly from the Christian Arab Community in Israel, now have a greater interest in biblical interpretation but for other reasons. Though they identify with their people who suffer daily in the West Bank and Gaza, they seek to have the mind of Christ and look for common grounds on which they could strengthen fellowship with the Messianic community in the Land and become a bridge of peace between the two peoples in the Land.

Lisa Loden in one of her comprehensive articles on this subject, quotes Rana Elfar, a Christian Palestinian who lives in Jordan. She claims that "due to cultural, historic and political factors, Arab

Christians have numerous difficulties with the Old Testament". On the cultural level, the Old Testament is often viewed as a Jewish book replete with stories of sexual immortality and not in keeping with the conception of a 'holy' God. Others view the Old Testament as being on the same level as the mythologies of other ancient Semitic peoples. "The political reality of the modern state of Israel makes it difficult for many Arab Christians, particularly the Palestinians, to even read the Old Testament, much less use it as a source of theology."[6]

In spite of the many Palestinian writers who do not use the Old Testament as a source for their theology, some still use it as integral part of the Bible, yet with a different approach than that of the Messianic New Testament. Some writers still use the Old Testament but selectively. The majority of Christian Arabs hold to a strongly spiritualized view of the Old Testament. In other words it is a spiritual hermeneutic. [7]

As was mentioned above, a person's hermeneutic is the outcome of an ethnic, personal experience, and national history. This is also true in a theological discussion between Messianic Jews and Palestinian Christians. Mitri Raheb, a pastor from Bethlehem, who has lived through the oppression, the sufferings, the closures and curfews, and at the same time has tried to maintain a Christian testimony, states his hermeneutic in this way:

> The persecuted understand the Bible differently from those who persecute. Those derived of power interpret it differently from those who possess power... When a Jewish concentration camp survivor speaks of 'the promise of land' and when an Israeli settler from the USA speaks of 'the promise of land', the same words have different meanings. The Bible, a book of persecution, has a crucified Lord as its centerpiece. It can only be correctly understood and interpreted when this theme remains in the center; it is our hermeneutic key.[8]

Naim Ateek and his entire devoted Christian family were displaced from their home in Bet-Shaan. In one night they lost their home and property and suddenly became refugees in Nazareth. In fact, the entire Arab community was expelled from the town where they lived and were replaced by foreign people who basically invaded their homes, moved in and took up residence instead of the former Arab population. Naim Ateek was a man who had served the Lord and his church for many years in Israel/Palestine. He has developed his theology out of such a history, personal experience and out of the suffering of his people. For him the Old Testament is the word of God, but he thinks that what is written in some books of the Bible is actually a development of how the Israelites understood the revelation of God. That revelation was fulfilled in Jesus. For Ateek the hermeneutical key to understanding the Bible and interpreting it is Jesus. He would reject any Old Testament text that contradicts the teachings of Jesus which promote love, peace and justice. Mrs. Loden says that Ateek's conclusions regarding the theology of the land arrive at an inclusive and universalistic view of the land, because anything else is repugnant and not reconcilable with his understanding of Christ's inclusive ministry and mission. It is a progressive hermeneutic.[9]

In various interviews with Christian Arabs who were born in Israel and still live in Israel, I found out that their hermeneutic is based upon their denominational affiliation. This is true among most of the older generation, and among the Brethren groups both youth and adults. This group bases their hermeneutic on a dispensational approach to the Land and eschatology. The current difficult political situation, the increasing aggression of the Israeli military and the prejudiced statements of some of the political leaders have a great effect on the Israeli Arab population. Christians as well as Arab Muslims living in Israel are included in those being affected by these developments. Younger educated Christians, have a hard time accepting the Messianic literal interpretation of the Land, and Israel as a fulfillment of prophecy. They are inclined to support amillennialism, replacement theology, or spiritualizing the Old Testament. For these people, Jesus is also the fulfillment and the reality of the shadows and typology of the Old Testament.

It is obvious that in addition to the political struggle which divides the two peoples of the Land, we see another conflict that divides the two parts of the Body of Christ. This conflict involves the divergent perspectives on the theology of the land and on eschatology that divides the followers of Jesus in the land. Because of the different hermeneutics, unfortunately there is a big gap between the two communities, theological division and lack of fellowship.

What should be done? Is there an answer? I think there is an answer, our common ground will never be hermeneutics, or political position. The answer is love (John 13:34) and obedience to His Commission (Acts 1:7, 8). We have a mandate from the Lord, in fact a responsibility of obedience to his great commandment of love, unity and commission.

The sufferings and tragedies which the Jews and the Palestinians experience daily demand consideration from every thoughtful and civilized human. It is time for the church in Europe to stand and act in a constructive way and contribute to the reconciliation between the two groups of the body of Christ. Unfortunately, the church in Europe in years past and the church in America today have endangered the very existence of the Palestinian church. It is about time to correct these mistakes and extend a hand and support for the edification of the Body of Christ in the land of Israel/ Palestine. Now is the time to work for a solution and reconciliation between Jews and Arabs in the land of Israel/Palestine. We live in a crucial time, worldwide, we all together, the growing community of followers of Jesus, Messianic Jews and Palestinian Christians in the land of Israel and the sister church in the West. Together we have a great responsibility to act as a bridge of peace between the two nations in the land, and through our unity and love for each other we can present a living model and testimony of coexistence in the land of Israel/Palestine.

For a conclusion I would like to quote my dear friend and devoted follower of Jesus Christ, Lisa Loden, who calls the Christian community in the land, Jews and Arabs alike, to approach any discussion of this topic in complete humility and brotherly love. Let us labor to 'keep the unity of the spirit in the bond of peace (Eph.4:3) until we come to the unity of faith' (Eph.4:13).[10]

Endnotes

1   Loden, Lisa, Peter Walker and Michael Wood, eds. (2000). *The Bible and the Land: An Encounter, Different Views: Christian Arab Palestinian, Israeli Messianic Jew, Western Christian.* Jerusalem: Musalaha, p. 23.

2   Ibid, p.35.

3   The covenant of Hamas, the Islamic resistance movement.

4   Skjott, B. F. (1997). "Messianic Believers and the Land of Israel – a survey," *Mishkan* 26, Jerusalem, 75.

5   Miller, David (1997). "Messianic Judaism and the Theology of the Land," *Mishkan* 26, Jerusalem, 31.

6   Stern H. David (1996). "The people of God, the Promise of God and the Land of Israel." Paper presented in Droushia, Cyprus on the theology of the Land.

7   Loden, p. 25.

8   Loden, p. 21.

9   Ibid.

10 Ibid, p.22.

10

The Doctrine of Election, the State of Israel, and "End-Times"

DAVID FRIEDMAN

1. The doctrine of election

At the beginning of my talk I would like to explore a vital question as to what the calling of God to the Jewish people is. In about 1700 B. C., my ancestors were chosen or called out by God from among all then extant people groups. This happened through a series of covenants that He Himself initiated. These covenants consisted of a group of repeated promises that were passed on from the historical figure of Avraham to his son Yitzhak, and consequently from Yitzhak to his son Yakov, and from Yakov to his sons. Let us quickly trace these events as recorded in the Torah. The covenant to Avraham promised him a number of things: the Land of Israel (Genesis 12:7, 13;14-15, 17; 15:18b, 17:8), growth as a clan/people group (12:2, 13:16, 15:5,7, 17:4-6, 18:18), and even suffering and dispersion as a people group in Egypt (15:13). Also promised were an honorable reputation (12:2b), and that Avraham would bless the world (12:2b). Last but not least was the promise of God to be a faithful God to Avraham and his descendants (17:7b-8).

The author of Genesis termed the animal sacrifice (15:13-18) combined with these promises as a "covenant" (15:18, 17:4, 17:7,9-11,14). The making of covenants was not a new phenomenon when God made this one with Avraham. Instead, we should see this as God using an already prescribed method of reaching a legal agreement with a second party. This covenant is irrefutably eternal in its time frame (17:7). The powerful, descriptive Hebrew phrase used here is 'berit olam'. Circumcision is the outward and eternal sign of participation in this covenant (17:11-13).

The promises of this covenant were passed on to Avraham's son Yitzhak, by God's choice (17:2,21; 21:12b). This did not mean that Yitzhak was inherently a better human being than Yishmael. It also did not mean that Yishmael was no longer a part of Avraham's family. In fact, I believe that the Torah teaches that he always remained in the family, but was not the inheriting son. Yishmael had his own set of promises given to him by God (21:13). But they were not the same promises as those received by Yitzhak in 26:2-5.

Messianic Jews are close to unanimous in understanding that the Torah teaches that Yitzhak also passed the covenant on to the next generation by giving it to Yakov, his son (28:1-4). The Hebrew words in these verses of promise to Yakov are the very same ones used earlier in Genesis. Genesis 26:3 clearly informs us that Yitzhak is receiving the same land promise that Avraham received. The Torah further teaches us that Yakov inherited these same covenant promises from Yitzhak (28:4a and 28:4b). These promises include a homeland, that God would be a faithful God, and that a population growth of the family/clan would occur; in addition, honor would be given to Yakov and his inheriting sons. These promises to Yakov are even referred to as "the blessing of Avraham(!)" (28:4).

Many Messianic Jews see our national calling as Jews, and as Messianic Jews as a subgroup, in the following two sets of scriptures: *"Now if you listen to my voice and guard over my covenant, you are a special treasure to me from among the nations; all the earth is mine! You will be to me a kingdom of priests and a separate, called-out nation..."* (Exodus 19:5-6, my translation).

In these verses, there is a call for Israel to be a nation of priests to the world, and to be a separated nation from the rest of the nations. The Bible's version of the role of a priest is given to us in the books of Exodus and Leviticus, as we learn about how the priestly tribe within the twelve tribes of Israel was to function. To summarize, the 'cohens' (priests) offered sacrifices on behalf of the nation, cared for the Temple/Tabernacle, and functioned in an intermediary and emissary role between the tribes and their God. The same word 'cohen' (for priest) is used in Exodus 19:5-6 to describe Israel's role among the nations of the world. Therefore, it was Israel's role, conceptually speaking, to be God's special emissaries and representatives to the world. As a sign of this, the priests annually sacrificed 70 offerings on behalf of all of the nations at the Sukkot festival. As well, the following set of verses pictures Israel in our priestly and emissary role:

"Look, I have taught you legal statutes and judgments that the Lord God has commanded to me. (You are) to carry them out in the Land that you will inherit. You will guard over them and do them, because the nations that hear about these commands will see your wisdom and your understanding. They will say, 'This people is a wise, understanding, great nation! For where is there another people as great, that has a God so close to them for all who call upon Him? And what other nation is so great as to have legal statutes and judgments that are so righteous, as this Torah (the one which I am giving you today)?" (Deuteronomy 4:5-8).

In the Deuteronomy text, Israel is called to be a nation that is a living reflection of God's righteousness. There is a call to strongly affect other nations, and all of this is conceived of happening in the Land of Israel.

The use of the Hebrew word 'olam' or 'ad olam' in the texts of the call and covenants show the perpetuity of Israel's call. As part of my PhD thesis, I did a study on the word 'olam'. It is used over 80 times in the Bible. In over 75 of its uses, it means "forever", i.e. as long as there is human history. Combined with Yeshua's statement in Matthew 5:17ff, many Messianic Jews believe that our priestly calling is an enduring one.

I believe that these two sets of scriptures expand and clarify my people's calling that is previously given in the covenant promises to Avraham, Yitzhak and Yakov. Thus I see the call of God to my people as *specific* and *enduring*, but *not exclusive*. These are important concepts to understand. By "specific", I mean this call to separation is to Avraham's flesh and blood descendants through his specific sons Yitzhak and Yakov. By "enduring" I mean that the call of God, resulting in the Jewish people being "chosen", is never cancelled. By "not exclusive", I mean that the call to the Jewish people is given to help insure *that all people* can believe in the One true God and in the Messiah. Thus, the call is not an end in itself, but a *means* that God conceived of to help further plans to redeem mankind.

Many people throughout history have not understood what the call to the Jewish people means. Too often this lack of understanding has had implications for the Jewish world: forced isolation and persecution of my people. This has been based on misunderstanding what it means to be called and chosen. Jealousy rose up and was perpetuated by influential persons in the early Church, and later in the emerging Muslim community. Both accused my ancestors of arrogance and pride in thinking that we were chosen above all other peoples by God. This faulty understanding of what it means to "be chosen" is still a theological factor in Christian and Muslim anti-Semitism today. We term its Christian expression as "replacement theology". Unfortunately, this idea of Christians taking the calling and blessings given to Israel was propounded by the early church fathers. One church father, Gregory of Nyssa (330-395), wrote: "Murderers of the Lord, assassins of the prophets, rebels and detesters of God, they outrage the Law, resist grace, and repudiate the faith of their fathers. Companions of the devil, race of vipers, informers, slanderers, darkness of the mind, pharisaic leaven, stone throwers, enemies of all that is beautiful." Origen (died 254) wrote:

> "Because of this, the things they did, they filled up the measure of their fathers not only in the blood of the prophets, but also in the blood of Christ ... as a result, the blood of Jesus is charged not only against those who actually did the deed but also against all generations of Jews afterward and forever. Because of this now and forever 'their house is left to them desolate'."

American Christian scholar Dr. Ray Pritz has noted:

> "Some pagan writers suggested that the conditions in which the Jews found themselves—poverty, defeat in war, temple destroyed, scat-

tered from their land—were because of evils they had done, a kind of punishment by their God. Christian writers continue with this idea, but now they connect the Jewish misfortunes to the death of the Messiah. And, of course, Christian writers can attach sayings from the biblical prophets to support their condemnation of the Jews. Ironically, this will only be mentioned in Christian writings after the cessation of persecution against the church in the fourth century. Before that time, the church itself was suffering many misfortunes, although no church father would have suggested that these misfortunes were because of evils done by Christians."

The idea that the temple was destroyed because of the death of Jesus was common in early Christian writings. It is still widespread today.

If there was covenantal failure on behalf of the Jewish people in fulfilling our priestly calling, what was the consequence? Did God know that at points in history, His called people would fail to be the light to the nations that He called us to be? Of course.

My observation is that the consequence has been that we have lost a vital part of our national identity and calling. To me, a Jew, this is sad. However, the story is not over, and I do not think that it is too hard for God to fix!

Let me burst a myth about my people's covenantal failures. This myth has caused many sorrows for my people in history. Many people write that the Jewish people are now displaced in every way regarding the promises of God *because we failed to believe in Yeshua*. The Christian church has done this and we call it "replacement theology".

The Muslim world has done this as part of their theological belief system, as well. The Qur'an states: "O you who are Jews, if you think that you are the favorites of 'allah to the exclusion of other people, then invoke death if you are truthful" (Sura 62:6). Again we see the replacement idea take hold in the Hadith [sayings of Muhammad and his associates that are not found in the Qur'an]: "The example of Muslims, Jews and Christians is like the example of a man who employed laborers to work for him from morning till evening. They worked till midday and they said, 'We are not in need of your reward.' So the man employed another batch and said to them, 'Complete the rest of the day and yours will be the wages I had fixed for the first batch. They worked up till the time of the Asr prayer, and said, 'whatever we have done is done for you.' He employed another batch. They worked for the rest of the day till sunset, and they received the wages of the two former batches" (Hadith Awqat Salah 533).

In both of these estimations, there is a simple equation: the Jews failed, so the Jews are displaced by Muslims. What the Muslim world has done, theologically speaking, is close to what the later Church fathers did in their theological reasoning.

But, *did* the Jewish people totally reject Yeshua? My friends, this is an historical myth. Let us look at the numbers: according to British historian Michael Grant, there were 8 million people in the Jewish world in the first century. Approximately 2 million of these Jewish people lived in Israel. Of these 2 million people in the Land at that time, a minority would have ever had the chance to hear Yeshua teach. Jerusalem had a population of around 100,000 people in the first century. Luke records in Acts 21:22, in about 60 A. D., that there was a strong, positive response to belief in Yeshua in Jerusalem. That text is worth studying in detail.

In this verse, Luke uses the word 'myriades' to describe the number of Jewish believers in Yeshua. This is a technical Greek word for a military division of 10,000 men. Luke puts the word into its plural form. In my studies of the writings of Luke, I have always read him as a careful and exacting historian. So, if we take him to be true to his words, he is telling us that at least 20,000 Jewish men of Jerusalem had responded positively to believing in Yeshua. I would think that some of these men had wives and children, but I will not guess at any such figures. Taking the least case scenario made by Luke's words, 20,000 people out of a city of 100,000 does not constitute a Jewish failure to respond. Anywhere in the world today, if 1/5 of a city population came to believe in Yeshua in a 30-year time period, Christians would term that a 'revival.' The Jewish people did not reject Yeshua wholesale. It is true that the political leadership of the Jewish people from his time period rejected him. But I do not believe that the text of the Newer Testament teaches that our entire people rejected him. History records that faithful Jews (like Peter, Paul, James, and *all* of the apostles!) spread the Gospel to the world.

The world should be grateful to God that so many Jews *did* accept, and then *did* share the message of our Messiah to the world. The opening of the door of the kingdom of Heaven was conferred upon Gentile nations by the Messianic Jewish leadership of Jerusalem (cf. Acts 15). God gave the Jewish people the knowledge of who Messiah was, but the Jewish people still had to determine the way in which to bring the Gentile nations into God's kingdom. That was done in a welcoming fashion, for which all Christian people should be thankful (to God, and at the risk of seeming impertinent, to my people, as well).

There is a further problem for those who embrace replacement theology: the Jewish people, Messianic and otherwise, didn't disappear from history. The miraculous birth of the Jewish state in our day and age is unexplainable in such a system of thought. If God rejected us, why would we still exist and be reconstituted as a nation, defying the norms of human history on both accounts? Even an agnostic skeptic like the 19th century American author Mark Twain could not figure out how the Jewish people still existed in his era. It simply defied reason: "The Egyptian, the Babylonian, and the Persian rose, filled the planet with sound and splendor, then faded to dream-stuff and passed away. The Greek and Roman followed, made a vast noise and they are gone. Other peoples have sprung up, and held their torch high for a time, but it burned out and they sit in twilight now or have vanished. The Jew saw them all, beat them all, and is now what he always was, exhibiting no decadence, no infirmities of age, no weakening of his parts, no slowing of his energies, no dulling of his alert and aggressive mind. All things are mortal, but the Jew. All other forces pass, but he remains. What is the secret of his immortality?" My suggestion is that God still has a role for my people to play in His plan for redeeming the world; thus, we are still around as a nation.

It has been the role of my people to shine God's light on the world. Looking back, I would say that we have partially succeeded in that call. If each of you could trace your personal human line as to how you became believers in Yeshua backward, there would be a faithful Messianic Jew standing at the very beginning; one who shared the message of his Messiah. Messianic Jews today believe that this national call of Exodus 19:5-6 endures today. In the future as well, the Torah shows my people functioning in this way. Rabbis and Jewish commentators throughout history have realized that our call is a call to responsibility. It is a calling to be a tool in God's hands. Our calling is not a source of pride or arrogance. According to the rabbis and teachers with whom I have studied, including Rabbi David Aronson, Rabbi Yakov Edelshtein and Rabbi John Fischer as well as from my own parents, our national calling is a *sober* calling. It is a call that endures much suffering. At some point in our lives, all Jews including Messianic Jews, repeat the words of Tevya the Milkman as he was addressing God in the story "Fiddler on the Roof": "Holy One, maybe You could choose someone else for once?" The entire Jewish world throughout history recognizes that we are called out to share a gift that we have.

Sometimes today the calling of the Jewish people is disputed because of seeming ineffectiveness. That is, critics will state that the Jewish people as a whole are not serving God, however this may be conceived of or defined. Therefore, we are not functioning as the kingdom of priests and the holy nation that God has called us to be. (One could also say the same thing about the church worldwide and throughout its history, but that is another story for another time).

As a national sports coach, I often liken our situation to that of an injured professional athlete. This athlete was once active, scoring points and contributing to the team's success. But now he cannot do so, due to his injury. He is inactive. After he heals, he will again return to being active, scoring points and contributing to his team's efforts. As an inactive team member, he is still under contract, and is part of the team. However, he is in some pain and cannot contribute to the game. Yet, his prognosis is excellent. The team expects him back in uniform very shortly.

Today the Jewish people are not fully functioning in the entirety of our national calling. But this does not cancel our calling, just as the injured pro athlete's contract is not cancelled by being injured. Given a world where for most of history, the Christian and Muslim communities have not allowed the Jewish people to function normally, if at all, what would one expect? Nevertheless, in His faithfulness, God will restore us fully "to the game" (cf. Zechariah 8:23, 14:16ff). Thus, I see us currently in a period of struggle attempting to return to our calling, a still valid calling. It will take God's revelation to us to help us understand our role and get into that mode of being (cf. Zechariah 12:10ff).

Why did God allow most of Israel throughout the past 2,000 years to not understand the value of Yeshua's life and death? There are few clues to the right answer given in the Torah. However, Shaul/Paul gives us some little insight into this question when he notes that: "...*hardness in part has happened to Israel, so that the full number of Gentiles may come in (to God's kingdom)"* (Romans 11:25). In Shaul's understanding, God was aware of the problem, and it did not defeat His purposes or His calling to Israel. Shaul again wrote: *"Did God reject His people? In no way!...Have they (Israel) stumbled that they should fall? Not at all!"* (Romans 11:1, 11). Shaul lets us know that whatever shortcomings exist in Israel's response toward God, that it does not mean the destruction of Israel and the cancellation of our calling.

We have few answers to the dilemma, but that is not a basis for inventing our own answers, or for putting one's self in the place of God and attempting to determine the fate of the Jewish people. God has already expressed His future plans: the redemption of Israel and of the world. Humans should fear lest they find themselves standing in the way of the unfolding of this miraculous plan (cf. Romans 11:20: *"Do not be arrogant, but fear (God)."* Questions will remain unanswered. Some Messianic Jews believe that unanswered questions are purposefully designed into God's plans of redemption. To quote a famous American professor as he reflected on why the Holocaust took place: "If God was silent, dare any of us speak?" I know it may seem that my people have fallen short of our national calling. Some people believe that this should be reason enough to take away our covenant promises and calling. But God does not fire the descendants of Avraham, Yitzhak and Yakov from a job, like a boss in the business world may do to his workers.

I know that I have spent some effort defending the validity of God's covenants and calling to the Jewish people. However, this is a major issue in the church world today. At a forum like this one, I can only hope that there will be serious consideration of the points that I have brought up regarding the covenants, Israel's national calling and its eternal validity. All other issues aside, this issue will determine how much of the Christian world behaves toward my people. Thus, I am very interested in emphasizing my points, and I thank the reader for his/her patience. Please understand that I do not make the above comments with any malice toward anyone. Yet I wanted to underscore what I feel are crucial points to make if one is to understand the role of the Jewish people, and the place of the country of Israel today.

2. The state of Israel

The question exists whether the current state of Israel fulfills God's purposes in prophecy. I can say that all Messianic Jews, in Israel and abroad, support the existence of the state of Israel. Messianic Jews are more supportive of a strong Israel with defensible borders than the broader Jewish community worldwide happens to be. So the Messianic Jewish community, worldwide, is highly supportive of historical Zionism, and of the struggle of our state today to defeat the well-known terror organizations that threaten our daily existence. This past summer, I wrote a position statement, adapted by the UMJC, supporting Israel's continual struggle to survive. The foundation for such beliefs is based on the Torah and on God's covenants. In addition, the majority of Messianic Jews would argue for the right of the Jewish people to an independent state in Israel based upon simple human rights; upon our UN approved mandate for such a state; upon our history, which has made us the most politically victimized people throughout the course of human history, with the gravest chapter in that story written here in Europe just a generation ago. Based upon the slaughter of 6 million European Jews ending just 60 years ago, most Messianic Jews would argue that the Jewish people deserved our ancient homeland as a refuge, and thus we are there in that capacity. The Messianic Jewish movement may be divided as to whether or not our modern state is the state pictured by the prophets, but even if that division is so, the great majority believe that the modern state *is indeed* the one mentioned in our Bible. All major Messianic Jewish organizations (the UMJC, the MJAA, and the two Israeli organizations with which I am familiar) believe this to be the case. I preface my short comments about whether today's state is the one prophesied in the Bible, because I truly do not know. Who can say for sure? However, I have a strong opinion that it **is** the very one talked about by the prophets, for the following reasons.

Many ancient cities that were destroyed have risen again in modern Israel (e.g., Isaiah 58:12, Ezekiel 36:10); the nation was declared ("born") in one day (14 May 1948; cf.Isaiah 66:8); Jews have returned from Russia (Jeremiah 16:15, 23:8), Yemen, Iran, Iraq, Syria (Isaiah 43:5), Ethiopia and South Africa (Isaiah 43:6). This multi-dimensional 'aliya' (immigration, return) has never before occurred in human history, especially during such a limited time frame as that in which it has occurred today. Such facts argue for a special consideration for the current state.

However, whether today's Israel is or is not prophesied, the Messianic Jewish movement is solid in its support of our right to live unharmed in our independent Jewish state, the same right that any other nation in the world possesses. Yet, at some point in time, the state of Israel, because it is filled with the descendants of Abraham, Yitzhak and Yakov, will indeed fulfill God's full purposes in prophecy. It may be a short while off; it may be a long while off. No one knows. That is up to God.

3. The end times
I wrote above that "There is a call [to Israel] to affect nations strongly, and all of this is conceived of as happening in the Land of Israel." Most Messianic Jews believe that events will unfold so

that this call is fully restored during the time of the return of Messiah Yeshua. Zechariah 8:23 will come to be, in light of the events of Zechariah, chapters 12-14. All Messianic Jews whom I have met believe that these scriptures have yet to happen. Other sets of verses are believed by Messianic Jews to be referring to the "end times". The phrase "end times" is a bit misleading, in that there is no such easily identifiable parallel term in the Hebrew Torah. The phrase most often used there is "aharit ha-yamim", which can be rendered "later days or last days", referring more *to an era* than an easy to identify short time period. (Indeed, Peter stated that we were in a "last era". It would be helpful to know what he was referring to! Cf. Acts 2:17, "en teis eschateis emereis").

Many rabbis have commented on the "last era of human history". The Talmud devotes 4 full pages to the subject of the times of the Messiah, and it parallels in many ways what Messiah Yeshua taught in Matthew 23. Most Messianic Jews take the words of Messiah Yeshua here to be instructive as to what the "end days" will look like, and use them as a blueprint for ideas about that era. I will leave it at that.

11

Western Restorationism and Christian Zionism: Germany as a Case Study

WILRENS L. HORNSTRA[1]

1. Two things, not one

Restorationism and Christian Zionism are two terms, and we are indeed speaking of two things here, not just one.[2] They deserve to be carefully distinguished, even though they overlap. Restorationism is first and foremost a theological idea and an expectation: as part of the *eschaton*, God will restore the Jews to the Holy Land. Its origin can be found in British Puritanism roughly around 1600. It is possible to draw political inferences from it, but for several centuries, not many people did this. Perhaps this is its most striking feature: apart from engaging in evangelistic outreach to Jews, the overwhelming majority of Restorationists have been remarkably passive. Even in 1948 and later, passive observation, not active support, remained the norm.

Christian Zionism, on the other hand, is anything but passive. For theological reasons, Christian Zionists ardently support the state of Israel. Already the name suggests a political and ideological dimension that is missing in Restorationism. Christian Zionism is much younger than Restorationism. It did not emerge as a coherent and recognizable movement until the 1970s. There were of course certain forerunners of the movement in the 19th and early 20th centuries, but they were not many, and someone who has studied the historical roots of Christian Zionism would probably know most of their names. For this reason, it seems not quite accurate to speak of a Christian Zionist movement for the period before 1970, with the possible exception of 19th-century England, where Restorationism became endemic and did lead to several political initiatives; but even there only a small number of people were activists.

In this paper, I will deal with the question of why this transition from Restorationism to Christian Zionism took place. I will also present part of an analysis of evangelical literature on Israel and the end times in German, because this analysis throws additional light on the developments of the past 60 years and on German evangelical perspectives on Israel. But before all of this, I want to present a three-dimensional model that attempts to explain Christian Zionism as a system of thought.

2. A three-dimensional model of Christian Zionist thought

The three dimensions are displayed in Fig. 11.1.[3] Obviously fundamental to Christian Zionism is its strictly literal hermeneutic. Together with its eschatology and its theology of the Jews as the people of God this makes up the foundational first dimension. It should be pointed out that Christian Zionism shares this foundation with Restorationism, and also that this literalist hermeneutic does not have to be dispensational.[4] After all, many Puritans and early Pietists held to both literalism and Jewish restoration long before dispensationalism.

The second dimension consists of the history of Jewish-Christian relations. This dimension is far more important to Christian Zionism than is commonly recognized, and not just in Germany (e.g. Brown 1992; Finto 2001; numerous German examples could be added). Christian Zionism can be a reaction to this past and to "replacement theology" (an often repeated phrase in Christian Zionist literature) as much as it is a reaction to the Middle East conflict. This second dimension forges a strong emotional bond with Israel and Jews, and adds substantial emotional power to the ideological narrative.

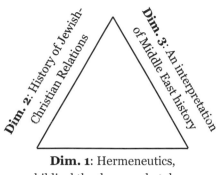

Dim. 1: Hermeneutics,
biblical theology, eschatology

Fig. 11.1: The three dimensions of Christian Zionist theology/ideology

The third dimension is a retelling of the history of modern-day Israel and the Middle East conflict which seamlessly connects 1917, 1948, and 1967 with biblical salvation history—Theodor Herzl, David Ben Gurion, and Moshe Dayan thus become part of the same biblical story as the Moses and David we learned about in Sunday school. The result is the transfiguration or sacralization of the state of Israel. It is striking how stereotypical the continuous reiteration of this history in numerous evangelical books has become. This is especially true for how this history deals with the Israeli-Arab wars and the origin of the Palestinian refugee problem, but there are numerous other elements that together make up this mythologizing retelling of history.

In a sense, these three dimensions are also three phases in Israel's history (Fig. 11.2). Dimension 1 represents the Israel of the Bible, dimension 2 the almost 2000 years of Jewish suffering and persecution climaxing in the Holocaust, and dimension 3 the restored Israel of the present. As such, the model represents a drama in three acts, which will shortly reach its culmination.

Judging by this model, Christian Zionism is a retelling of the biblical story which appears to be as much Israel-centred as it is Christ-centred. As a result, Israel becomes the key to understanding the

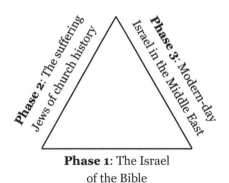

Phase 1: The Israel
of the Bible

Fig. 11.2: The three dimensions as three phases in Israel's history.

world, it is seen as a champion worthy of emulation and adulation, and thus Israel functions as a central symbol of the Christian faith. At this point, I want to add a word of criticism. It is this theological aspect of Christian Zionism which I find most disturbing. In my view, it contradicts the essential ethnic universalism of the gospel. Guided by a pre-Christian reading of the Old Testament prophets, it condemns the Jews to be special, different, and separate at least until the second coming and probably far beyond. For all its good intentions, I do not think that this does the Jews a favour.

The ethical question is important and controversial as well, but it is perhaps more easily debated. Was Israel in the right in 1948, in 1967, in 1982, in 2006? This is arguable, and it is in principle possible to discuss the history, the politics, and the ethics of these events. But this becomes far more difficult if those involved consider Israel a central symbol of their faith. This makes it much harder to have an open discussion about those central symbols. As soon as a discussion begins it quickly feels as if someone is touching the apple of your eye, and I think this explains the intensity of Christian Zionist reactions when confronted with criticism of Israel or with theological alternatives to Christian Zionism.

3. Personal turning points: three gateways

The three dimensions of the model also represent three gateways through which people can come to embrace a Christian Zionist perspective. There are of course many who have come in through their fascination with the end times. This is the case for Hal Lindsey and Tim LaHaye, and in Europe for someone like Wim Malgo of Midnight Call. The latter has published numerous books and magazines in many languages, most of them filled with a highly speculative and apocalyptic reading of biblical prophecy, at every turn connecting this with events and developments in the present (as of his writing), especially when they had something to do with Israel. This has made them so dated that hardly any of Malgo's books are still in print, a mere 14 years after his death; it is painfully obvious that his forecasts were usually wrong.

Although eschatology is an important element in most versions of Christian Zionism, it is by no means always the leading motivator for those involved. Interestingly, leading Christian Zionist organizations have on occasion downplayed the importance of this dimension for their commitment to Israel.[5]

There are others for whom the confrontation with the German or Christian past vis-à-vis Jews played a major role. Their response can in part be understood as a form of repentance and a desire to make up for the terrible treatment of Jews in the past. In Germany, there are several individuals and organizations for whom or for which this dimension is of special importance: Harald Eckert, *Ruf zur Versöhnung* (Call to Reconciliation), the Evangelical Sisterhood of Mary, and others.

As for the Sisterhood of Mary, it is of particular importance, because it was so early to embrace a Christian Zionist stance and also because it has exerted significant influence worldwide, in spite of its small number of members. Founded in 1947 by Basilea Schlink, the Sisterhood's special concern for Israel dates back all the way to 1955.[6] Already in 1957, the first sisters went to Israel to serve in Israeli hospitals and old people's homes. Also in 1957, the Sisterhood first published the *Israelgebet* (Israel Prayer, Schlink 1995), a confessional and intercessory liturgy for the Jewish people, which it used for a weekly service on Friday evening, the beginning of the Jewish Sabbath, for a number of years. In 1961, the Sisterhood founded a home, Beth Abraham, in Israel for Holocaust survivors as an expression of repentant love and a sign of reconciliation. Schlink's first and most important book on Israel, *Israel / My People*, also appeared early, in 1958, a time when few evangelicals were writing about Israel other than in the dispensational abstract, as a component in their eschatological scenario. It is also worth noting that the book begins not with eschatology, but with German—and Christian—guilt due to the Holocaust. In this unequivocal confession of German and Christian responsibility for the Holocaust, Schlink was ahead of her time, especially among German evangelicals. However, her deep concern for the Jewish-Christian past went hand in hand with strong partisan support of the state of Israel. *Israel / My People* already contains typical elements of later Christian Zionist literature, such as Israel's miraculous victories over the supposedly vastly superior Arab armies, and a lack of concern for Palestinian refugees (Schlink 1967:22, 91-4).

The Jewish-Christian past is also a central concern for the Christian Forum for Israel, a platform founded by several Christian Zionist organizations in 2002 to cooperate and to coordinate their activities. It explicitly lists dealing with guilt towards the Jewish people resulting from the past as one of its aims. Since evangelicals are a small minority in Germany, approximately 1.6 per cent of the population, the Forum for Israel has limited political influence. Nevertheless, because of Germany's sensitive political culture in relation to Israel, German politicians still take note. In addition, the unified front of the Christian Forum makes it an important voice in the evangelical movement, especially in charismatic-Pentecostal circles.

A third gateway into Christian Zionism is a confrontation with the re-established Jewish state and the miracle of Israel; it is for good reasons that many Christian Zionist organizations offer tours to Israel. Such a confrontation can have a powerful effect. One prominent and early example of this is the neo-Pentecostal Bible teacher Derek Prince, who happened to be in Israel-Palestine during the

War of Independence in 1948. The events convinced him that he was witnessing the fulfilment of prophecy. It gave him a head start over other Pentecostals, and Israel has been an important topic in his teaching ever since.

Another example is Ludwig Schneider, a former Pentecostal pastor from Germany. Schneider was in Israel during the Yom Kippur War. On his return, in 1973, he founded the organization *Israel-Hilfe* (Israel Aid). Since this is even earlier than Bridges for Peace, which was founded in 1979, it makes *Israel-Hilfe* one of the very first organizations with a purely Christian Zionist objective. The organization grew rapidly, but in 1979 went bankrupt in the midst of financial chaos and scandal. Schneider and his family took refuge in Israel, where he founded a news agency, *Nachrichten aus Israel* (News from Israel, NAI), and eventually published a monthly magazine in German and English sent from Israel, filled with news and information from an unequivocal Christian Zionist perspective.[7]

Of course, these three paths are not mutually exclusive; often, two or all three dimensions play a role. However, it shows that the dynamics leading to a fully developed Christian Zionism are diverse; to turn a passive Restorationist into an active Christian Zionist takes more than just dispensational eschatology.

4. The collective turning point

The previous section explored how individuals may come to embrace Christian Zionism. For the evangelical movement as a whole, it has already been pointed out that in relation to Jewish restoration and Israel, passivity was the norm; an activist, Christian Zionist movement only began to emerge in the 1970s.[8]

Passivity gave way to activism, and Restorationism gave birth to the Christian Zionist movement, in response to the Six Day War of 1967, the Yom Kippur War of 1973, and other events related to the developing Middle East conflict. To many evangelicals in the West, Israel's victory in the Six Day War was a miracle of truly biblical proportions, and could only be explained as a direct intervention by God. To understand the state of Israel as a miracle and a prophetic sign of the end was certainly not a new idea, but the 1967 war did much to make the idea "sink in", and move it from the level of theory to that of deep personal conviction. But then the Yom Kippur War and a range of other events and developments made clear that this miracle was threatened and in need of support, Israel became a cause which many evangelicals embraced with the same vigour that they have demonstrated in missions, evangelism, and various reform and aid projects.

An interesting illustration of the impact that the Middle East crisis was making on German evangelicals is the following declaration issued by the German Evangelical Alliance (EA) on 4 December 1974:

> In a time of increasing isolation of the state of Israel by the peoples of the world, the board of the German Evangelical Alliance stands by Israel's right to exist [*Lebensrecht*] within secure borders in the land of its fathers.
>
> The governments of the nations see themselves forced through the so-called oil weapon of the Arab states and by ideological movements to take a pro-Arab position against Israel.
>
> The board of the EA calls upon all members of the church of Jesus to recognize the biblical aspects of these events. God is acting today with his people Israel, to whom he has promised the land of its fathers.
>
> We are convinced that the Middle East crisis cannot be solved through terror and military actions. In the conflict of Israel with the Palestinians we pray God for a solution that makes possible for both the people of Israel and the Palestinians the full development of their lives.
>
> In this hour of increasing pressure we call for intercession and for financial aid for Israel. At the same time we see that the Arab peoples also stand under a promise of God (Is. 19:19-25), in which a peaceful coexistence of all peoples in the Middle East unto a blessing for the whole world has been pledged.[9]

The declaration is Restorationist, particularly in the third paragraph, and could easily be understood as an expression of Christian Zionism. However, it should be interpreted in its context: this was 1974. At that time oil-producing Arab states were putting pressure on other countries to distance themselves from Israel. Among leftwing intellectuals in the West, sympathy and partisan support for the Palestinian cause increased dramatically after 1967. This produced an anti-Zionism that could be no less ideological than the more extreme forms of Christian Zionism. In addition, the relationship between the German and Israeli governments, warm during the 1960s, cooled down considerably in the 1970s. The statement is thus a reaction to perceived one-sidedness and unfair bias against Israel, rather than the expression of an ideological commitment. Whether the perception is accurate or not is, of course, a matter for debate, but if one accepts it, the statement is not unreasonable.

It includes what I think is a real and sincere—although perhaps naïve—attempt to do justice to both sides in the conflict. The title of the article in which the declaration was published, "Intercession for Israel and the Arab Peoples", already bears this out, as do the two final paragraphs, which acknowledge the Palestinians and even express faith in a special blessing for the Arabs.

The statement is therefore not as Christian Zionist as it may appear at first sight. Besides, it did not exert any lasting influence; I have not found **any** reference to it. The EA never again published an official statement on the Middle East conflict. In contrast, it has taken a clear stance on the issue of Jewish evangelism and Jewish-Christian relations (Deutsche Evangelische Allianz 1999), which continues to be available both in print and on the Internet.

Clearly, the EA did not persevere on the path of its 1974 declaration, nor did it follow up with the kind of ideological hardening that can often be observed in Christian Zionism. But many others did, and the declaration illustrates the kind of concerns that led them into this direction.

5. The development of Christian Zionism as reflected in Evangelical literature

In order to provide a different perspective on these and subsequent developments, I want to present some of the results of a book analysis included in my thesis (Hornstra 2006: Chapter 5). A significant part of my research project was an analysis of the almost 400 evangelical books published in German since 1945 which deal with Israel, the end times, or both.

All of these graphs divide the period under consideration into units of 5 years on the X-axis. Fig. 11.3 shows the development in the number of titles published for the first time during each 5-year period; this number is divided by the nationality of the author (German, American, Israeli, or other). The graph shows an overall increase in the number of titles published, although this is probably not meaningful; most subjects experienced such an increase in number of titles published. I have included this particular graph to show, first of all, that American translations only began to play a role after 1969, and second, to point out the pronounced dip in the late 1980s. I will come back to this dip.

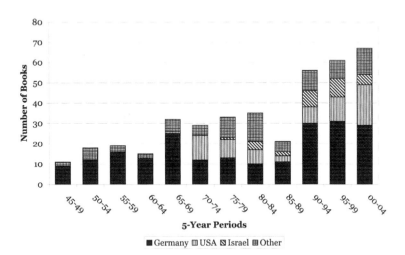

Fig. 11.3: Development in number of books first published in a given period, divided by nationality of author (cumulative).

Fig. 11.4 shows an interesting shift that has occurred. I have classified these books by whether their predominant interest was eschatology or Israel. "ee" stands for predominantly eschatological, "ii" for predominantly dealing with Israel, "ei" and "ie" stand for books that pay attention to both subjects, but more to one than to the other. The Y-axis shows the percentage of these classes for each 5-year period. The shift from interest in the end times to interest in Israel is quite pronounced.

A similar picture emerges when books are classified according to the strength of their Christian Zionism. Fig. 11.5 shows this development in relative terms. Type 1 and 2 are Restorationism, Type 4 is a highly apocalyptic form of Christian Zionism (many of these books were written by Wim Malgo), Type 5 and 6 are the most Christian Zionist.[10] Again, the development with time is quite pronounced. Fig. 11.6 shows the same picture, but in absolute numbers. Here, we can once again recognize the dip in new titles during the late 1980s. We can also see that the books published before and after this dip differed in kind: Type 1, 2 and 4 were dominant before the dip, Type 5 and 6 became dominant after the dip.

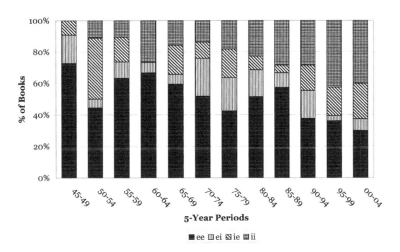

Fig 11.4: Relative development in end-time (ee, ei) and Israel books (ie, ii).

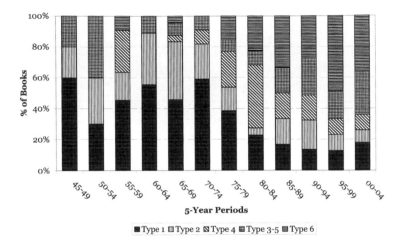

Fig 11.5: Relative development in Restorationist and Christian Zionist books (Type 1-6).

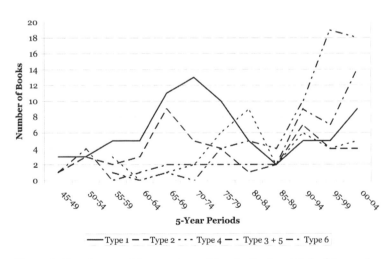

Fig 11.6: Development in number of books first published in a given period, divided by type of Restorationism and Christian Zion ism (Type 1-6).

In other words, the increase in titles dealing with Israel and the end times took place in two waves that are fundamentally different from each other. The first wave was to a large extent driven by interest in prophecy and the end times; this is the "prophecy boom" of the 1970s. The second wave, which still continues today, is Israel-driven.

What this means is that interest in Israel has clearly increased with time at the expense of purely eschatological publications. This development went hand in hand with an increasingly Christian Zionist stance, an increase that of course parallels the increase in the number of Christian Zionist organizations. This suggests that at least some of today's Christian Zionists are less determined by eschatological considerations than were their predecessors in the 1970s.

One more aspect of this analysis is worth noting here. The total number of evangelical titles for the entire period that argue for an alternative position, that is, one that is neither Zionist nor Restorationist, is 12.

6. Differences between Germany and the United States

In light of this fact it may surprise you to hear me make the following assessment, but I nevertheless think it accurately captures the German situation.[11] Many German evangelicals, especially those who are theologically and politically more aware, would shrink from a fully developed Christian Zionism.[12] They definitely display an attitude (attitude, not ideology) which is pro-Israel, and they may habitually speak of "solidarity with Israel". Such people may or may not be Christian Zionists. However, even if they are, they are not necessarily blind to the human dimension of the issues, and they are both willing and able to consider these. The 1974 declaration discussed above illustrates this comparatively moderate position.

Yes, there are also ideologues for whom this is not true. But there is considerable diversity among evangelicals and even among Christian Zionists, as well as between different countries. Before drawing out the implication of this as a word of conclusion, let me list a few of the differences I have noticed between Christian Zionism in Germany and in the United States.

- For obvious reasons and not surprisingly, Germans show more interest in both the German and the Jewish-Christian past.

- Dispensationalism is far more important in American Christian Zionism than it is in Germany. Too often, Christian Zionism and dispensationalism are treated as virtual synonyms.[13] This may be largely true for the United States, but it is certainly not true for Germany and other nations. One result of the book analysis introduced above is that those books that most strongly advocate Christian Zionism are often the least explicit on dispensationalism and the most likely to include statements that contradict the dispensational system. At the same time, a number of German dispensationalists, while certainly pro-Israel, have not fully embraced Christian Zionism. A good example is Ernst Schrupp, who for many years was the leader of the Wiedenest Bible School, the most important training institution of the Brethren movement in Germany. One would think it could not get more dispensational than that. But Schrupp's Restorationism never crossed the line into a full-blown Christian Zionism. One important reason for this may well have been that Schrupp was in touch with both real Palestinian Christians and with real messianic Jews in Israel.

- German evangelicals seem somewhat less apocalyptically minded. There is less of the extremely speculative kind of popular eschatology. Especially Pietist authors and leaders, although usually wed to a traditional premillennial eschatology, show reluctance to engage in overt speculation.

- Another significant difference is that the spectrum of theological views on Israel is narrower in Germany than in America, Great Britain, and the Netherlands. There are few alternative, non-Zionist voices among evangelicals, and none of them are institutional.

- Overall, I would say that most German evangelicals do not display the kind of militancy common in American popular evangelicalism, and this also affects their perspective on Israel. It should be added, however, that this relative moderation does not apply to those who have fully embraced Christian Zionist ideology to become "true" Christian Zionists; they are frequently no less militant than Christian Zionists elsewhere.

7. Rightly dividing Christian Zionism

There is, therefore, considerable diversity among evangelicals and even among Christian Zionists on the question of Israel. For practical purposes, this is an important point. An accurate portrayal is crucial in criticism and debate. No one will take seriously a critique of his position that is based on a distorted or one-sided portrayal of that position.

The recent "Jerusalem Declaration on Christian Zionism", a wholesale condemnation of Christian Zionism as false teaching, colonialism, imperialism, and militarism by four Middle Eastern bishops and patriarchs, is a case in point. This may be true for some Christian Zionists, but many others will not recognize themselves in this portrayal. The response, a joint declaration by BfP, CFI, and the ICEJ, is—at least on this point—not much better.[14] It maintains the illusion of a monolithic movement by producing a categorical statement of what Christian Zionists do and do not believe. It fails to admit that at least part of the criticism is true for at least some Christian Zionists, if not for many:

> Christian Zionists do not base their theological position on end-time prophecy, but on the faithful covenant promises of God given to Abraham some four thousand years ago. They do not have a "thirst for Armageddon," and do not claim to know the sequence of events that will lead to it.[15]

Really? All Christian Zionists? I have read too much material that does exactly what this statement denies. Anyone who has read John Hagee will realize this denial lacks credibility.

Two declarations have been issued, but I am afraid no communication has taken place. Let me therefore close with a word of practical wisdom from Stephen Covey, which may help us regardless of where we stand on Israel and Palestine. It is one of Covey's *Seven Habits of Highly Effective People*, and it really applies to us all: first seek to understand; then seek to be understood.

Endnotes

1   Wilrens Hornstra presents excerpts from his 2006 dissertation. The complete text of the PhD dissertation is available at www.christianzionism.de. The author can be contacted at wilrens@sbsgermany.de.

2   I should also point out that Christian Zionism is not simply a form or variety of Zionism in general. As a movement, an ideology, and a theology it is quite distinct, although Jewish *religious* Zionism and *Christian Zionism* have a number of things in common, and in many cases seem to get along well. This, however, is a recent development; the two Zionisms have separate origins, and are not two varieties of one movement.

3   Although it is beyond the scope of this paper, I should at least mention that there is a fourth dimension, at least in charismatic-Pentecostal circles, which leads to a distinct variety of Christian Zionism. For a discussion of this variety and its features, see my thesis (Hornstra 2006: section 6.8), which can be downloaded at www.christianzionism.de.

4   For this, see especially David Parsons (2005), who in a paper published by the International Christian Embassy Jerusalem (ICEJ) explicitly distances himself from dispensationalism.

5   See David Parsons (2005), as well as the recent response to the "The Jerusalem Declaration on Christian Zionism" by Bridges for Peace (BfP), Christian Friends of Israel (CFI), and the ICEJ (Brimmer et al. 29.8.2006).

6   '40 Jahre Israelauftrag' 4.1995, *Was geschieht auf Kanaan und drau-βen?* 2-4.

7   The English edition appears under the name *Israel Today*.

8   There is substantial literature documenting both the overall passivity of evangelicals and the 1970s as a turning point (e.g. Ariel 1991:88-91, 94, 121; 1992:442f, 446, 449; 2002:16; Halsell 1989:72-4, 178; Merkley 2001: 37, 40f; Railton 1998:171-89; Sizer 2002:83, 96; Weber 2004:212f; Wilson 1991:xxv-xlii).

9   "Fürbitte für Israel und die arabischen Völker" 9.12.1974 *idea* /47:II. An English translation was published five weeks later, but since it is far from perfect, I have here included my own; "Board of the German Evangelical Alliance Holds Autumn Meeting" 15.1.1975 *idea* /2:6.

10 Type 3 proved rare and was therefore included in Type 5; for more details, see my thesis.

11 Significant evidence for this assessment is presented in Chapter 4 of the thesis, in the form of an analysis of Israel-related articles in *idea-Spektrum*, the news and information magazine associated with the EA.

12 As is probably true elsewhere, Christian Zionism in Germany is strongest and spread most widely in charismatic and Pentecostal circles.

13 In his book on evangelicals and Israel for instance, Timothy Weber (2004) speaks throughout of dispensationalists.

14 Both statements are included in Brimmer *et al.* (29.8.2006).

15 *Ibid.*

References

Ariel, YS. *On Behalf of Israel: American fundamentalist attitudes toward Jews, Judaism, and Zionism, 1865-1945.* Brooklyn: Carlson Publishing, 1991.

—. "In the Shadow of the Millennium: American fundamentalists and the Jewish people" in Wood 1992: 435-50.

—. *Philosemites or Antisemites? Evangelical Christian attitudes toward Jews, Judaism, and the state of Israel.* Jerusalem: Vidal Sassoon International Center for the Study of Antisemitism, Hebrew University of Jerusalem, 2002.

Brimmer, R, Sanders, R, & Hedding, M. "A Defense of Christian Zionism: In response to the bishops' declaration", 2006. www.icej.org/article. php?id=3464 Accessed 7.9.2006.

Brown, ML. *Our Hands Are Stained with Blood: The tragic story of the "church" and the Jewish people.* Shippensburg: Destiny Image Publishers, 1992.

Covey, SR. *The Seven Habits of Highly Effective People.* New York: Simon & Schuster, 1999.

Deutsche Evangelische Allianz (ed.). *Zum Verhältnis von Christen und Juden: Eine Handreichung der Deutschen Evangelischen Allianz.* Stuttgart: Deutsche Evangelische Allianz, 1999.

Finto, D. *Your People Shall Be My People.* Ventura, CA: Regal Books, 2001.

Halsell, G. *Prophecy and Politics: The secret alliance between Israel and the U.S. Christian Right* (rev. edn). Chicago: Lawrence Hill Books, 1989.

Hornstra, WL. *Christian Zionism among Evangelicals in the Federal Republic of Germany.* Dissertation (PhD), Oxford Centre for Mission Studies and University of Wales, 2006.

Merkley, PC. *Christian Attitudes towards the State of Israel, 1948-2000.* Montreal: McGill-Queen's University Press, 2001.

Parsons, D. "Swords into Ploughshares: Christian Zionism and the battle of Armageddon", 2005. www.icej.org/news/swords.pdf. Accessed 18.1.2005.

Railton, NM. *The German Evangelical Alliance and the Third Reich: An analysis of the "Evangelisches Allianzblatt".* Bern: Peter Lang, 1998.

Schlink, MB. *Israel/ mein Volk.* Darmstadt-Eberstadt: Evangelische Marienschwesternschaft, 1967.

—. *Israelgebet.* Darmstadt-Eberstadt: Evangelische Marienschwesternschaft, 71995.

Sizer, SR. *Christian Zionism: Historical roots, theological basis & political consequences.* [CD-ROM] Dissertation (PhD), University of Middlesex and Oak Hill Theological College, 2002.

Weber, TP. *On the Road to Armageddon: How evangelicals became Israel's best friends.* Grand Rapids: Baker Academic, 2004.

Wilson, D. *Armageddon Now! The premillenarian response to Russia and Israel since 1917.* Tyler: Institute for Christian Economics, 1991.

Wood, D (ed.). *Christianity and Judaism: Papers read at the 1991 summer meeting and the 1992 winter meeting of the Ecclesiastical History Society.* Oxford: Blackwell, 1992.

Reconciliation between Women in Israel/Palestine

LISA LODEN

1. Context

In today's Middle East, Israelis and Palestinians are engaged in a complex, lethal struggle that directly affects the entire population of the area. The conflict not only involves the conflicting factions, but in today's global village, it has implications for much of the world.

The two sides of the conflict view it from quite different vantage points. Even within the Jewish community there is no one factor upon which all agree. On the Jewish side, certain elements maintain that the conflict dates from patriarchal times and is prefigured in the enmity between Jacob and Esau, Isaac and Ishmael. Others describe the source of the conflict as Islam's view of conquest and land. Those who hold these views see a combination of theological, historical, and ethnic elements as sources of today's conflict. Others in the Jewish world describe the current conflict as yet another manifestation of anti-Semitism while some maintain that the causes are solely political and relate primarily to issues of land and water.

On the Palestinian side there is greater consensus as to the source and causes of the current conflict. In the main, Palestinians see the situation in terms of occupation and land-based disputes. They view the conflict as recent, dating from the end of the nineteenth century when Jews in significant numbers began to immigrate to Palestine. These immigrants found an existing Arab population in the territory to which they had moved. Increased Jewish population and economic viability stimulated immigration to the area by Arab peoples from the neighboring nations. With Israel's victory in the 1948 War of Independence, the conflict took on new dimensions that laid the foundation for the current conflict based on land and occupation.

There is agreement between all parties that the conflict has affected the entire population living in the area. On the Palestinian side, large numbers have been displaced, land has been confiscated, families have been separated, villages have been relocated, and homes have been demolished. On the Israeli side, the threat, as well as the actuality, of random acts of terrorism has traumatized the entire population. The fact of mandatory universal military conscription has profoundly affected generations of Israelis. There has been much loss of life and injury on both sides. Fear has played a major destructive role in the subsequent breakdown of relationships between the two populations.

The populations are severely distanced from one another. Cultural and social, economic, religious, and political differences are all factors that contribute to the distance. Palestinian Arabs are oriented towards a more rural, traditional Middle Eastern life style whereas today's Israelis are heavily influenced by the Western urban experience. Language is another factor since both Hebrew and Arabic are spoken along with various other languages of the immigrant population. Ethnically, however, Jews and Palestinians are closely related. Recent genetic testing has shown that Israeli Jews and Palestinian Arabs are genetically closer to each other than either group is to any other ethnic group.

The overwhelming majority of Israelis are Jews who see their attachment to the historical land of Israel as rooted in the patriarchal narratives of the Bible. Most Messianic Jews hold to this understanding. Palestinian Christians claim their spiritual heritage from the time of the early church. History, however, shows that Islam swept the Middle East in the 8th century causing most Christians in the Middle East to become Moslems. Today there are viable congregations of Palestinian Christians and Messianic Jews who live in the midst of the majority Moslem and Jewish populations. These groups are numerically small. In total, Arab Christians of all kinds constitute about 3% of the population of Israel/Palestine. Messianic Jews constitute approximately 0.1% of the Jewish population of Israel.

Dating from the time of the British Mandate in Palestine, Christian missionaries were sent to evangelize the Jewish population of Palestine. This mission work was met with great resistance and as a result, many of these endeavors were refocused to outreach to the more hospitable Arab communities. Consequently, Christian mission in the "Holy Land" has focused on one group to the exclusion of the other. The effect of this singular focus has not been helpful to the parties in conflict.

In the Israeli/Palestinian spiritual arena, theology has played a great role. Regarding the place of Israel, supersessionism has been the dominant theology of the Palestinian church and Liberation Theology is strong in some sectors. In the Israeli sector, most Messianic Jews identify with dispensationalism and affiliate with the Christian Zionist agenda.

In contrast to the Messianic Jewish community which is entirely evangelical, Palestinian Christians are denominationally quite diverse. Anglicans, Lutherans, Latin Catholics, Greek Orthodox, Syrian Orthodox and other traditional Eastern Orthodox denominations make up a large portion of the Palestinian Christian community. These groups tend to relate to international denominational and ecumenical bodies. In so doing they frequently adopt a liberal agenda that focuses on issues of human rights at the expense of an evangelistic mandate for all. For them, the most prominent issue is justice. Reconciliation between the communities of faith on both sides of the conflict is not a priority.

The Messianic community sees concerns for truth, meaning their own understanding of biblical teaching regarding the place of Israel, as primary. This focus often precludes any motivation for reconciliation with Palestinian Christians who interpret scriptures about Israel differently.

2. Activities

The reconciliation activities addressed in this case study have been taking place between Palestinian and Jewish women who are believers in Jesus. The reconciliation activities described here are between the Palestinian evangelical community and the Messianic Jewish community. Although both groups are minorities within their peoples, these two faith communities stand firmly within their ethnic groups and identify with their respective struggles.

Organized meetings between Palestinian Christian and Messianic Jewish women began in the mid 1990's. These meetings have continued on an annual basis since that time. As an outcome of the annual conferences, during the past two years, small groups of women have been meeting several times throughout the year.

The initiative came from Musalaha, a ministry of reconciliation that was founded in 1990. Women meet together to tell their stories, listen to one another, learn about each other's lives and communities, pray and worship together. These activities have been chosen to enable the women to begin to get to know each other and to build bridges of understanding and trust. All of the participants, speakers and those attending have been from within the two communities.

From the beginning of these meetings, the basis has been clearly defined as meeting together "in Christ/Messiah." The primary spiritual identity has always been stressed and the commonality of faith emphasized. Women tell their stories, speak from a personal perspective as wives, mothers, and daughters; each struggling to live a life of faith in the midst of conflict and tension. Biblical passages focusing on the unity of the Body of Messiah are highlighted as foundational for reconciliation as are the scriptural exhortations to love one another. Listening to the personal narratives of one another in the light of sharing a common faith has been crucial to the encounters. Speaking from the heart rather than from an intellectual perspective is always a characteristic of these gatherings. Corporate prayer for common concerns has been a significant unifying factor. Singing together in one another's languages has also been another important unifying element.

In the early years, women shared about their cultural traditions in the context of their life of faith. A positive aspect of the women's meetings has been the participation of only local women. In the diverse cultural/religious milieu of Israel/Palestine this has been particularly enriching.

Musalaha has provided financial subsidies to enable these meetings to take place. Both communities struggle economically and women would be unable to attend such overnight meetings if there were no financial aid given. The administrative staff of Musalaha has handled administrative matters but the conference/meetings are planned and organized by a committee of women on a volunteer basis. All of the participants come voluntarily.

Frequently these meetings have taken place during times of active conflict between the two communities. This has meant that local military authorities have had to be petitioned for permission to allow Palestinian women to leave their areas and travel to the other side where the meetings were being held. The context of violence still contributes to the urgency and importance of the meetings. One such meeting was held on the eve of national elections in the Israeli sector and it was at this meeting that united prayer for common concerns was particularly poignant.

3. Outcomes

The purpose of the women's meetings has been to begin a relationally based process of reconciliation. There have been both short-term and long-term outcomes of the reconciliation meetings between women.

In the short-term, the feedback from women attending the meetings has been almost entirely positive. They relate that they have been personally enriched and challenged by the faith of other women living in vastly different circumstances. In the context of the meetings, stereotypes have given way to seeing each another as sisters and distance has given way to mutual embrace. Worshipping together has been described as "a taste of heaven." Comments like "why did I wait so long to come to these meetings?," express the short-term impact of these gatherings. Feedback from the women repeatedly contains a desire for more frequent gatherings.

In the longer term, as a result of these meetings, relationships have begun that have endured through times of accelerated conflict and violence. One of the long-term outcomes has been a number of ongoing relationships, first between the women themselves, then between families and in some cases between two congregations. The level of contact between the two groups evidences this. There are frequent telephone contacts, particularly during times of violence, as the women call one another to encourage and support each other during time of crisis. Families visit one another and attend congregational meetings together. As an outcome of the recent smaller meetings, a monthly email prayer fellowship has been formed. This functioned well for several months but has not yet maintained the level of continuity that is hoped for.

The witness of the united community of faith that includes Jews and Arabs has had a positive effect on those hosting the meetings. These meetings have at times been held in commercial venues and staff and other guests have expressed amazement at seeing "enemies" embracing each other. In their respective communities, the existence of loving relationships "across the lines" is challenging and it is a witness to the power of Jesus to break down walls.

Some criticism has been leveled against Musalaha's reconciliation activities among women by Palestinian Christians who are not a part of the evangelical community. The focus on common faith rather than on issues of justice and liberation is perceived as naive and an avoidance of the "real" issues. Another criticism is that rather than empowering women to stand for justice, these activities lull them with a false sense of harmony between opposing sides in the conflict.

In the context of the Israeli/Palestinian conflict, it is clear that there is a strong connection between reconciliation and evangelism. The reconciliation spoken of here is within the community of faith where Messianic Jews and Palestinian Christians are beginning to express that they are one in Messiah. Women seem to be initially more constitutionally suited to exploring relational issues than men.

They naturally identify in solidarity with other women, regardless of other superficial differences. These women strongly connect with one another on an emotional basis. The fact of friendship across the lines powerfully witnesses to the only One who has the power to unite and reconcile such diverse people into one family.

4. Analysis

The context of the Israeli/Palestinian conflict has ongoing implications for reconciliation activities. Palestinian women have a much more difficult time getting out of their communities than do the Israeli women. In earlier years, it was legally possible for Israeli women to go into the Palestinian territories while Palestinian women have always needed to have permission from the military authorities to cross over into Israeli territory. Few Israeli women have been willing to confront the military presence and cross the border to the Palestinian territories. It is much more difficult today than when the reconciliation activities were initiated. Obtaining permission to enter Israel is very difficult for the Palestinian women and in most cases they are refused entry permits. In December 2006, for the first time in three years, five women were allowed to enter Israel for a Musalaha conference. When the separation wall is completed, sometime in 2007, it will be even more difficult for Palestinian women to come into Israel. Not all Palestinian women are willing to illegally cross over into Israeli territory.

The positive short-term outcomes that were described in the previous section have occurred because of a basic willingness to meet with one another on the ground of commonality rather than difference. Although differences are recognized, they are not the focus of the meetings. The meetings are intentionally structured so as to encourage the participants to see beyond the differences of culture, ethnicity, theology and language. The clear focus has always been the unifying fact of the commonality of salvation in Jesus held by both communities.

The dominant party in the conflict is the Israeli presence. In the reconciliation activities, however, Arab participation has always proportionally outnumbered Jewish participation. As the years have passed, this balance is slowly changing, as more Jewish women are willing to be involved in the activities. This is in large measure due to the positive short-term impact of the annual women's meetings. The Messianic Jew has felt herself a part of the dominant group and as such has not felt the same vulnerability or need to interact with the other side. In reconciliation activities, the inequality of the parties comes quickly to the fore and this at times threatens the self-perception of the Jewish participant.

In order to facilitate the meetings, venues have to be chosen that are both accessible and non-threatening to both sides. At times this has meant that some of the Palestinian women were unable to obtain permissions to attend the meetings. As these circumstances are beyond the control of the organizers, there is no way that such problems can be avoided. They are however a significant factor in reconciliation activities in the Israeli/Palestinian conflict.

As women meet together on the basis of faith, with the aim of building trust, this leads to deeper relationships and commitment. This has proved to be an effective method of reconciliation. In particular, communal worship and prayer for common concerns of the gospel, family and society are important elements that have proved to be valuable tools in the ongoing process of reconciliation between the two communities.

While there are similarities between reconciliation activities in many parts of the world, reconciliation in the context of the Israeli/Palestinian conflict is in some ways unique. In the area of women's work, the model described in this case study can be applied in other contexts of conflict. There remains, however, one issue that is unique to this conflict and to the context of reconciliation within the larger community of faith. This is the issue of the place of Israel in the plan of God. Israel cannot be dismissed by adopting a supercessionist theology of the people of God, however well reasoned it may be. The "one new man" continues to be made up of two reconciled parties, Jews and non-Jews. Ultimately all reconciliation initiatives and activities in the Israeli/Palestinian context must somehow deal with this thorny issue.

Reconciliation is finally about family. Restoring the family of God, healing it from the effects of sin and brokenness that have damaged relationships, both human and divine, is the heart of the gospel. Relationship building within the family of God is but the first step to seeing the healing of the world's brokenness.

13

Christ is Our Hope

AZAR AJAJ

One of the most used words in Israel is 'peace'. We read about it in the newspapers, politicians promise peace and we all hope to have it. But we find that peace is far away from us. Instead of peace, our world is full of violence, hatred and revenge; more now than any time before.

I grew up in this situation, the situation of hatred and enmity, of wounded hearts and suffering people. As a citizen in this country, I always wondered if there was any hope that we could ever live in peace. As I was growing up I thought that the solution should be a political one, and for some time I put my hopes in the politicians, but soon I discovered that peace does not come through these people. A turning point in my life was when I started to understand that as a Christian I have a role in bringing hope to the hopeless. I was fully convinced that God wanted to use his body, the believers in this country, to do so. Through the love, respect and the peace that we have with each other in the body of Christ (Jewish and Arab believers), we can bring hope to our people.

My main challenge was that in order to have this relation with my Messianic brothers, I needed to get to know them. For this reason, fifteen years ago, I was more than happy to take part in the Musalaha conference where Christian Arabs and Messianic Jews went on a desert trip for few days. We were away from the hustle and bustle of life, facing together the desert challenges and difficulties, singing together, laughing together, sharing our hopes and prayers for a better situation in our region, and above all making the effort to understand the fears and the suffering of each other. We sought to respect one another, and to understand that we can be one, and we can have peace together, in spite of our differences. That was not easy. What was required from all of us was humbleness, self denial and a willingness to pay the cost.

I left the conference thinking that this step of meeting Jewish believers and trying to build bridges with them was only one step on a very long road, but as a Christian I was fully convinced that this was the only road I could walk. This road is the road of reconciliation, love and acceptance of my Jewish brothers and sisters. I praise God that this conference was not the last one for me. My family and I have had the privilege of taking part in further meetings. It has been great to see how God has been working in our hearts, and showing us that it is possible to live in peace together through the peace we have in Jesus Christ.

My relationship with Jewish friends started with Musalaha, but it did not stop there. What these programs did was to motivate me to be more active in making the effort to build relations together. It is true that in every step I took I discovered that we are different, but also I believed that we can still enjoy our unity in our diversity, and we have no other choice but to be one, because "He is our peace, and He is our reconciliation" for that we can be one, and together we can bring the real hope of the real peace for our nations.

14

Witnessing to Religious Jews and Palestinian Muslims: Perspectives from the Book of Acts

PETER F. PENNER

Is it appropriate to speak about Christian witness during a conference that deals with the issue of the Israeli-Palestinian conflict and asks how Christians should respond to it? Is not part of the problem in the Middle East, and particularly in Israel/Palestine, the way in which Christians interpret biblical texts and the fact of Christian missions throughout 2000 years?[1] For many people the attempts of, especially evangelical, Christians to send missionaries into the region and to lead Palestinian Muslims and religious Jews to Christianity are very offensive and amount to nothing more than proselytizing. Many in the Christian West deny the need of organized missionary activity toward the Jews and Muslims and reject evangelism as unhelpful.[2] Are religious Jews and Palestinian Muslims not already believers in the same God of Abraham in whom Christians believe? Contrary to some in evangelical Christianity, I would like to affirm that Jews, Christians and Arab Muslims are Abrahamic in their origins (even though "this term does not describe them adequately or completely" (Hinze and Omar 2005:71)) and believe in the same God. Jews have an obvious ethnic relationship to Abraham, Christians have claimed the spiritual legacy of Abraham for themselves, and Arab Muslims (though this is disputed by some) descend from Abraham through Ishmael.

All of the Abrahamic faiths have in their belief systems a place for Jesus of Nazareth. He may not be recognised by religious Jews as Israel's Messiah,[3] but he is accepted as someone coming from within the Jewish faith and some would acknowledge him as a Rabbi. In the Muslim faith Jesus is recognised with the title of a Messiah, even though great differences are evident in how Jesus' person and mission are perceived. Because of these differences, Christians and Muslims have debated his identity and role since the rise of Islam (cf. Solomon, Harries and Winter 2005). Whenever Christians testify to Muslims about Jesus, they do not bring Christ with them, he is already known at least in some way within Islam. Mark S. Kinzer in his book on *Post-Missionary Messianic Judaism* argues that even through the twenty centuries of history after the coming of Yeshua/Jesus to his people, he was with the Jews, especially in their suffering, which is similar to his on the cross (2005:213-233). Nevertheless both religious Jews and Palestinian Muslims need to expand their understanding and have a Pentecost experience with the Messiah through the Holy Spirit. A conversational dialogue between the faiths needs to happen in the process of witnessing to the Messiah, so that the Messiah would lead religious Jews and Palestinian Muslims to reconciliation between each other as well as inside each group. Could this nourish the hope for peace in Israel/Palestine?

What role should Christians who come from outside of the region play in the witness process? What role could followers of Jesus play who identify themselves with Jews (Messianic Jews) and Palestinians (believing Christians)? There is a minority of Jews who clearly identifies with Judaism and at the same time recognises Yeshua as the Messiah of Israel. At present their number in Israel comes to about 10.000 while worldwide we find about 100.000 Messianic Jews.[4] They are often not recognised by traditional Christian churches and often find themselves under pressure from their own fellow Jewish neighbours. Still, they maintain their witness to the Messiah among their people. Approximately the same number of

Palestinian Christians live in the region of Israel/Palestine.[5] They are often neglected not only by historic churches, but also by some evangelical groups. Most of these Palestinian believers' communities originate from historic churches in the region. Some arrogant Christians, especially in conservative evangelical circles outside of Palestine, fail to recognise that the origins of Christianity in this region can be traced to the early days of Christianity as referred to in the book of Acts. But very few in these communities have a background in the Muslim faith and are not so called MBBs (converted from Islam).

If the Messiah Jesus is a last hope for the region—as evangelical believers, Jews and Palestinians alike, think—what keeps Muslim Palestinians from crossing the border to Christianity and what needs to be done in terms of contextualising the Gospel to lower the barriers? Religious Jews seem to have similar difficulties as Palestinian Muslims in becoming followers of Jesus the Messiah. We can point to the Messianic Jewish community that has grown in the last centuries, but it has primarily attracted those Jews who were already uprooted from the Jewish faith, community and tradition. Many who have joined the messianic community in the last 15 years have their origins in secularised Central and Eastern Europe (Kjaer-Hansen and Skjott 1999:13). What are the difficulties for religious Jews in accepting Yeshua as their Messiah? Is it that God himself has hardened the hearts of religious Jews or Palestinian Muslims, as some claim when referring to their view of some New Testament texts using church history? Or could it be that Jews have rejected the Messiah of Constantinian/Hellenistic Christianity and as a result have been replaced by it as chosen nation?[6] Do Muslims really worship the God of Abraham? Some western groups question this fact, trying to prove that Muslims, in fact, worship the enemy of the Jewish and Christian God.[7] Much has been written on these issues and questions which I, in no way, want to repeat or even summarise. My modest attempt in this article is to follow believers in Jesus/Yeshua in the Middle East, who clearly disagree with the present western view, and explore ways, possibly through deeper contextualisation, in which the Gospel can more successfully penetrate circles of religious Jews and Arab Muslims (See John Travis 2000:53-59).

Also, I would like to move beyond this discussion and emphasise the call of Christ to continue a witness to him as Acts 1:8 calls the disciples to do. In order to design biblical contextualisation I would like to point out some parallels between Acts and current groups and situations and invite us to learn from the narrative theology of Acts about the early Christian witness to the Abrahamic faiths: Jews and Samaritans. As we go back to the Acts of the Apostles, we cannot ignore the history and relationships between the three Abrahamic faiths. As we try to learn from Luke's models of witness, we may need to look at the history *after* Acts and how we can read it in light of events narrated in Acts. To do this in a short article means, at most, to initiate a conversation and to offer some impulses for the issue.

1. Samaritans, Arab/Palestinian Muslims and the Messiah Jesus

While we recognise that many texts in the Bible emphasise that Jews are the people of God, it seems that we can find only slight information on Palestinians and Muslims.[8] To perceive them to be the group identified in the Bible as Philistines, as some have chosen to do, may be possible but does not help much for better relations with the Jews. Recent attempts to draw parallels between the Samaritan story in the Scriptures and the story of Arab Muslims in their relations to Jews may prove more beneficial, if we try to learn from the difficult relations between Samaritans and Jews in Biblical times for the *current* difficult relations between Palestinians and Jews (Masri 2006:49ff.). An evangelical group in Lebanon has recently formulated this option in order to enable a fresh look at the tensions that have quite a bit of nourishment not only on ethnic but also religious grounds.[9]

The Samaritans play an important role in the history of the Jews since the kingdom of Northern Israel disappeared in exile and a new nation called Samaritans emerged as a neighbour of Judah (2 Kings 17:24-41: *people of Samaria*[10]). History speaks of difficult relations between Jews and Samaritans from the first mention of this group in Ezra 4 and Nehemiah 2:1ff.. The words Samaria and the Samaritan(s) appear more than 120 times in the Bible. As told in the Bible narrative, this is a long history between two difficult neighbours, similar to the present relationships between Jews and Arabs. Old Testament as well as New Testament background studies provide many examples where tensions and military actions were the way in which the two nations had related to each other ever since the exile. It had not changed much from the time of Ezra to the times of Jesus.

The Samaritans claimed that they were Israelites, a faithful group that had maintained true worship throughout the various changes of worship places and rites during the time of Joshua and the judges (Anderson and Giles 2002:10-13, based on the Samaritan historian Abu'l Fath). Shechem, where Joshua gathered the tribes of Israel for a covenant renewal before his death (Josh. 24:1), became the place of worship for the Samaritans while Jerusalem (and not Dan, Bethel or Shiloh—all important cultic centres in early Jewish history) eventually became the place of worship for Jews. In their opinion, "the question of origins should be directed more toward Judaism than to themselves" (Williamson and Evans 2000: 1057). The Jewish account from the Old Testament, on the other side, links Samaritan origins to Assyrian conquests and their colonizing efforts in settling people onto Jewish soil who then also adopted the faith of Israel (2 Chr. 30; 34:6; Jer. 40:5). Josephus offers some additional information about the links between Jews and Samaritans. According to him (*Antiquities of the Jews* 11.8.2), when the priest Manasseh was expelled from the high priesthood in Jerusalem because of a foreign wife whom he did not want to divorce, Sanballat of Samaria, his father-in-law, built a temple for him on Mount Gerizim to continue with his priestly duties. It seems that many other priests, attracted by Sanballat's financial gifts, joined him which resulted in a scandal in Jerusalem. Scholars disagree on various issues as to the origins and development of the Samaritan nation and we cannot present the discussion here in full.[11] What seems clear is that since Ezra's times we find this ethnic group worshipping the same God whom

Jews worship but at Mt. Gerizim instead of in the Temple. According to Josephus (*Antiquities of the Jews* 12.7.1.), Samaritans were fighting on Antiochus' side against the Jews during the Maccabean revolt, increasing the already strong oppression from occupants, and causing further rejections to any relations with them. They even asked to have their temple renamed in honour of Jupiter Hellenius, a Greek deity (12.5.5). But this is somewhat in tension to other available information.

Samaritans, similar to the Jews, were people of the book. The Samaritan Pentateuch with its minor differences from the Hebrew Torah was the only text of the Hebrew Bible that they accepted. They also honoured the prophet Moses. In recent studies on the Samaritan faith, scholars find that, similar to the variety of streams and parties among Jews, during the time of Jesus there was also a diversity of groups and sects in the Samaritan context (Williamson and Evans 2000:1059).

We can easily find parallels between Jews, Christians and Muslims similar to the parallels we find between Jews and Samaritans. They are all called Abrahamic and the Hebrew Bible, the Old Testament, is part of the common tradition of all three. Christians and Muslims have other issues in common, similar to the Jews and Samaritans. Jesus is of key importance for both. Because of this specific role of Jesus/Isa, both faiths have the hottest debate exactly on this issue. The relation and origin of the three—Muslims, Jews and Christians—are complex and tense as is or was the relationship between Jews and Samaritans. To analyse how Jesus and the preaching of his disciples about him has changed these relationships may help us to find ways to overcome the tensions between religious Jews and Palestinian Muslims. Religious Jews just as Palestinian Muslims oppose, though in different ways, the Christian Messiah. This similarity between Jews, Muslims and Christians is also the reason for the tension as this closeness points to divisive roads between the three, similar to what happened between Jews and Samaritans. All these commonalities in tension provides a parallel to the difficult relations between Jews and Samaritans. So we will look at how the tension between Jews and Samaritans was illuminated as people from both groups became followers of Jesus.

Arab Islam claims, similarly to the Samaritans,[12] that its faith goes back as far as Abraham and his son Ishmael, which has some ground in the Hebrew Bible and makes Jews and Arabs relatives.[13] It seems somewhat problematic to draw parallels between Arab Muslims and the Samaritans of Jesus' times because the former appeared so much later than the latter. One can, for example, perceive Mohammad as an Old Testament prophet who calls the Arab nations back to God and to devout following of their father Abraham,[14] except that Mohammad appears more than 500 years after Christ. With a *chronos* perspective on time we have difficulties to place him into the Old Testament. But we may need to look at the encounter of Mohammad with his context not from a *chronos* but from a *kairos* perspective, which may change our view of Islam and its prophet Mohammad. When affirming a parallel between Samaritans and Arabs, as we did earlier, we meet the other problem that both ethnic groups still exist and are clearly separate. Both nations are still monotheistic. This article, however, does not attempt to draw ethnic lines, but rather to compare some parallels in relationships as one finds them during the time of Jesus between Jews and Samaritans and today between religious Jews and Arab Muslims, and here particularly in relation to Palestinian Muslims.

Against this background, it will be interesting to look at the Jewish-Christian-Samaritan encounter in the Gospels and Acts and apply it to the Jewish-Christian-Muslim encounter. The Gospel of John narrates an incident between Jesus and the Samaritan woman that may help us to draw some conclusions about how Jesus would act in a similar situation such as currently exists between Christians and Muslims. In the same Gospel, Jesus himself is accused of being a Samaritan. So it is of importance to look at this text in John 4:1-43 in order to interpret Acts 8:1-25.[15]

1.1 The Samaritan Woman (John 4:1-43)

The region of Samaria was not the best place for Jews to travel in order to get from Galilee to Judea and Jerusalem. Many preferred the longer way on the east bank of the Jordan River, because they could expect violence from those living in Samaria on the west bank. Josephus refers to some of these tensions (*Antiquities of the Jews* 20.6.1 and *Jewish Wars* 2.12.3). But the shortcut for Jesus' travel leads through Samaria and the text clearly indicates that Jesus purposefully went through this region with a clear agenda (Morris 1971:255). Keener summarises the events of John 4 in this way: "Jesus crosses strict cultural boundaries separating races (in the general sense of culturally distinct peoples), genders and moral status, pointing to the new and ultimate unity in the Spirit" (1993:271). Even though Jews and Samaritans had much in common, as demonstrated above, theological, ritual and, even more, historical issues separated the two nations, as we read in the response of the Samaritan woman (John 4:9).

John introduces us to the situation by telling how, most naturally, the disciples are on their way to buy food as all of them are hungry and thirsty after a long trip. It is mid-day, and John loves to portray exact place and time settings for the different conversations. The theme is quite comparable to John 3: the same offer is extended by Jesus to a Jewish educated nobleman Nicodemus as well as now to a simple lady from Samaria (Senior/Stuhlmueller 1984:289). In this setting the living water is the key to the conversation (Schneider 1988:111). The conversation, moving from water to the Samaritan-Jewish controversy about the place of worship, and finally from the prophet to the Messiah, is a step-by-step self-revelation of Jesus to the Samaritan woman and to the reader (Schnackenburg I, 1965:456). The climax of the conversation, as it has been prepared by the story development, is to see the Christ whom the Samaritan woman finds in Jesus.

Reading Samaritan sources as well as present scholarly literature about the Samaritan faith, it is difficult to prove that they expected a Messiah as the Jews did. At most they expected a prophet like Moses (Williamson & Evans 2000:1059; Keener 1993:273,341). This is probably not what the Samaritan woman refers to when she identifies Jesus as a prophet. John's Samaritan woman does know about a Messiah who needs to come, and it seems that Jesus has no questions about what God Samaritans worship. Early followers of Jesus can point to a number of Samaritans who believed in Jesus and we find historic proof that a number of early Christian communities existed on Samaritan territory. Possibly one particular group inside of the Samaritans was more prepared to interpret Taheb as a Messiah, but we have no proof of it, beside that this text lets a simple Samaritan woman speak about a coming Messiah. Williamson and Evans (2000:1060) believe that "if historical tradition lies behind the saying, its present expression must be regarded as a Johannine paraphrase for his more Jewish-orientated readership." But this is just an attempt to bridge the tension between what we know about Samaritans and what we find in John.

Verses 20 and 21 bring the long-winded conversation to an issue important for our study. Some claim that the story here connects to the account of 2 Kings 17:24–41 and to the way in which the origin of Samaritans was defined traditionally. Tenney believes that not only the place of worship is discussed but even the possible syncretism that happened after the Northern Kingdom disappeared and in the process of colonialisation foreign deities were mixed with the ancestral God of Israel (1981:56), a similar conviction that some Christians have about the Arab Allah. Jesus points out that the right sources come from the Jews and indicates he is the Messiah also coming from the Jews, but does not question that the same God is worshipped in both places.

However, when pointing to the future, he clarifies that both places, Mt. Gerizim as well as the Temple in Jerusalem, will lose their significance as cultic centres. After the approaching passion event, both Jews and Samaritans will be able to address God as their Father, because Jesus revealed God to Jews, Samaritans and all nations (Schnackenburg 1, 1965:470). This means that both, Samaritans and Jews, will through the Messiah be brought into a deeper relationship, understanding the gift of God (Schnabel 2002:262) and worshipping one God, in the Spirit of God. An important dimension is presently missing on both sides: the Spirit of God, who will bring them into right relations with and worship of God. As Acts demonstrates, the same Spirit did bring them into unity, as part of the calling to be Christ's witness (Acts 1:8). Through the Acts 2 Pentecost experience in Jerusalem as well as through the Samaritan Pentecost in Acts 8 Jesus' words become true. Coming back to the topic of the conference, this seems to be the experience that both nations, Jews and Palestinian Muslims, need in order to make way for reconciliation and peace.

1.2 Philip, Peter and John in Samaria (Acts 8:1-25)

We can easily connect the story of Acts to John 4 as one of the many early historic sources of Jesus' interaction with Samaritans. We can also assume that, similar to the situation in Judea and Galilee, during Jesus' lifetime there already were communities of Jesus followers in Samaria (Schnabel 2002:658). Our text in Acts does not refer to such groups but rather presents a story that in the end integrates Samaritan believers in Jesus with the Messianic Jewish community in Jerusalem.[16] The story under consideration follows after Stephen's long speech and his violent death. Some scholars argue that Stephen had a Samaritan background as his references to the Pentateuch during the speech seem to follow the Samaritan version of it.[17] This is possible; even so it raises questions. If Stephen is a Samaritan believer in Jesus, then he is in good company as in the group of deacons elected in Acts 6 we also find a proselyte from Antioch (v.5).

Samaria seems to be a natural place for those under persecution to flee to from Jerusalem, as are Judea and probably Galilee. Is this because there were already some links from Jesus' times? Luke may have picked up the story of Acts 8 directly from Philip's own oral retelling, but does not provide any link to the earlier ministry of Jesus. Instead, it is clearly a story that prepares the church and the reader for a much more extensive barrier crossing, a Jewish Christian mission reaching out to Gentiles (Pesch I, 1986:270-271). The step toward the hated Samaritans was for Jews a very difficult one, and so it was initiated by Hellenistic Jews, such as Philip. These Hellenistic Jews were in the primary focus of the Jerusalem persecution and they were better prepared to cross seemingly insurmountable cultural barriers (Longenecker 1981:357).

In this story we also encounter Simon the Magician, who is an interesting Samaritan character and plays an important role in the narrative. Identifying him, Justin Martyr believes he was found in the city of Gitta where Philip preached (1.26).[18] Others suggest the rebuilt city of Samaria, called Sebste (Schnabel 2002: 660). Keener suggests Neapolis, on the site of the ancient Shechem, as the place of action (1993: 344). Traditionally Sycher is perceived to be the city where Philip went and where the conversation between Jesus and the Samaritan woman took place (Longenecker 1981:356-357). But Luke does not give us any details for the identification of the exact place, as it seems to be of no importance for his theological narrative.

The main story does not place Jewish scripture and beliefs against those of the Samaritans, but against a possible saviour personality: Simon the Magician, who pushes himself to the centre,[19] against Philip who is presented as the messenger of Jesus the Messiah. Simon possibly stands for end time prophets such as Dositheus, who also live in the early first century and played an important role in the story of the Samaritans (Williamson and Evans 2000:1059). It seems, as we have discussed already, that the Samaritans expected a prophet like Moses (Dt. 18:15) This would mean that the early church confronted people who took a divine or messianic role in the Samaritan population, while accepting the Samaritan scripture or liturgy.

At the centre of the power play in Acts 8 is Jesus Christ who is preached to the Samaritans, followed by miraculous signs. Both, the good news and the miraculous signs, led to expressions of happiness, as the competition presented by Luke continues (Pesch I, 1986:273). Luke clearly describes Simon as having a better starting position, because he comes from within the culture and is in direct opposition to Jesus and not to Philip who is simply the messenger (Schnabel 2002:659). But, surprisingly, Samaritans believe the gospel of the kingdom of God, preached by Philip, and he baptizes all who respond to the Gospel. But the story again takes a surprising turn: only when the apostles Peter and John arrive and lay hands on them, do they receive the Holy Spirit (Acts 8:15,16).

Luke paints a parallel story here to the story of the Jewish Pentecost and to the Cornelius story. On the one hand, it demonstrates that Samaritans receive the same Spirit as Jews when they believe in Jesus the Messiah. On the other hand, Luke shows that, as the apostles come, lay hands on the Samaritans and identify with them as part of the same movement, the Holy Spirit brings together two similar groups who believe in the same God of Abraham but live in constant tension with each other. Later Samaritan literature supports the links between early Christianity and Samaritans (Anderson 2002:274-5,295,301,339-340).

Acts 8 is clearly a fulfilment of Acts 1:8 where Samaritans are specifically listed as those to whom the witness of the disciples is directed. The Pentecost is repeated here, if we read it from the *chronos* perspective. But if we read the same story from a *kairos* perspective, the same quality of experience happens in Jerusalem, Samaria and Caesarea (Schnabel 2002: 660). During the time of persecution Jewish believers in Jesus found in Samaria not only a place of safety but also good soil for the Gospel of Jesus, who brought peace and reconciled all humanity with God and with each other. Acts 9:31 echoes this and observes that after the local persecution *"the church throughout Judea, Galilee and Samaria enjoyed a time of peace. It was strengthened; and encouraged by the Holy Spirit, it grew in numbers, living in the fear of the Lord."* Many years later in history we find Arabs offering safety to Jews under persecution from Christendom. The developments before and after the establishment of the state of Israel after the Second World War changed these relations drastically toward tension and violence.

1.3 Arab Muslims believing in the Messiah Jesus

There are many Muslims who believe in the Messiah Jesus, and we can point to many miracles and wonders accompanying situations when Muslim Arabs find Jesus as their Messiah and experience a dramatic conversion similar to that of Saul/Paul on the Damascus road. But very few of them have maintained their cultural and social, especially family, relations after such a conversion and most of them have never been able to witness to their friends and relatives in the same way as the Samaritan woman did after her "conversion experience" when meeting Jesus. The story in Acts teaches us about ways in which some Samaritans came to faith in Jesus as the Messiah and how this parallel can be continued today. Is it possible that Messianic Jews have a responsibility to witness to Palestinian Muslims about Jesus as the Messiah of both, Jews and Palestinians, a Messiah who is able to bring together people who have hated each other in the past, Jews and Samaritans of old and Jews and Palestinians today, making them one people (Eph. 2)?

Important insights can be drawn from Acts 15, the main contextualisation effort of the early church, for ways to contextualise the Gospel to Arab Muslims, and in this instance, Palestinians. The following study of Jewish Christianity will help us to look at Jewish mission throughout the Acts of the Apostles and especially at the first century and later the Messianic Jewish movement. But as we analyse this movement, I would like to raise a question here about whether it is possible for Arab Muslims to develop a Messianic Muslim movement as Messianic Jews have developed a Messianic Jewish movement. We will return to this debate toward the end of the article.

2. Christian witness to the Jews

The Christian mission to the Jews is a very controversial issue, as referred to in the introduction, and it is a key problem that disturbs Christian-Jewish relations.[20] It is against this background that many in the larger Christian community position themselves against any Christian mission to the Jews. We will find this explicitly not only among historic churches and the World Council of Churches, but also implicitly among evangelicals, for the same or for different reasons. Others argue that, because Israel had lost its role as the people of God and the church had gradually replaced it, a distinct mission to the Jews had already been dropped in the book of Acts specifically by Paul. After the birth of Pietism and during various mission activities starting with the end of the eighteenth century and ending before the First World War, known as "the first period of modern Jewish missions", some attempts have been made to evangelize Jews, with some success but also with problems in contextualising the gospel (Robinson 2000:521).

A second phase has been identified with movements such as the Jews for Jesus in the early 1970s and with the development of a Jewish Messianic movement that is now some 30 years old. There is much more concern for contextualisation and for allowing Jewish believers to follow religious practices and beliefs that are very similar to the first century Jewish Christian movement, also known as *The Way or the Nazarenes*. These Jewish believers claim to have "dual citizenship in that they are part of the remnant of Israel and they are the Jewish wing of the church" (Goldberg 2003:111). Robinson (2000:522) believes that some 0.5 % of Jewish people belong to this group (2000:522), while others estimate up to 1 % of Jews. This number includes many coming from Central and Eastern Europe.[21]

Much has been published recently on this development, and many experts have presented this movement from different sides.[22] It is not the purpose of this article to look at the Messianic movement, besides recognising it as at least partially successful, even though it seems controversial to some. Our main goal is to look at New Testament sources, particularly at the praxis of Acts, in order to learn from the early Christian mission among Jews and by Jews. An issue that goes along with that development and is also debated using the New Testament is the issue of the Land, as emphasised by most Messianic Jews together with dispensational groups, claiming Palestine as the Promised Land of Israel. It is interesting to recognise that neither Christ nor the apostles speak about the Land, even though it may be connected to the issue of the kingdom, as it is raised by the disciples in Acts 1:5. The issue of the Land is debated in various articles of this book.[23]

Replacement Theology has also surfaced as a major question in this conference and is debated in different articles. In many discussions it seems that there is an either/or position. Israel's role, as some argue, has to be in unity with the global church (Ephesians 2:11-22) and, in some sense, it sounds as if Jewish Christians must join Hellenistic Christianity, rather than the opposite. But early

Christianity seems to have had the opposite view, as Christianity grew out of Judaism. Supporting neither of these positions, I agree with Yee's conclusions on Eph. 2:11-22 and on the new entity/unity that Christ creates: "The Jewish 'body politic'... is so confused with Israel that the Gentiles could hardly become part of it... The idea of the 'one body', which the author introduces to rectify the exclusive 'body politic', is not a replacement of Israel but an anti-*politeia*... rather than a new entity outside Israel" (Yee 2005:222).

Twenty centuries of Christian history offer more than just the two positions that come up especially in the evangelical context: dispensational or reformed. An honest reading of the New Testament seems to indicate that both systematic approaches press the biblical text beyond its actual meaning. As I move on with the discussion of Jewish mission, I would like to maintain the tension between a special role of Israel and of Christianity as the new Israel.

2.1 Mission to the Jews and the early Jewish Christian Mission

God's initiative early in the Old Testament determined that Jews were part of the covenant. There was no need for a mission to the Jews, and some may add that there is still no need (Fisher 1982:4). But in a *missio Dei* sense, there was God's mission/outreach to Israel and the Jews. His messengers (angels and prophets) were his missionaries who saved Israel from Egypt and called Israel to follow God's commandments and take responsibility to live according to the standards of God's chosen people. It is in this way that Jesus and his disciples take on the role of missionaries to the Jews.

On the other hand, there was the responsibility for Israel to be included in the *missio Dei* as an agent of God, a missional people for the nations. Fisher writes: "While there is no sense of missionary outreach in the Hebrew Scripture, there is clearly a sense of universal witness. Israel is to be a light to the nations (Is. 49:6) as well as a blessing to them (Gen. 12:2; 17:6; Sir 44:21)" (Fisher 1982:4). This double mission has its later parallels for the church: to be a new agent in God's world and at the same time be an object of God's mission.

Rabbinic tradition clearly points to the role of Israel as an agent of God's mission in witnessing to the nations. *"You are my witness, says the Lord"* in Is 43:12 to mean that *"when you are my witness, I am God, and when you are not my witnesses, I am not God"*, Cohen comments quoting from Midrash Tehilim on Psalm 123:2 (Cohen 1982:64). This connects the witness to God and Israel's role to the nations. The source of Israel's mission is the Torah. Israel first needs to see it with its blind eyes (Is. 42:7) in order to correct its own behaviour but then, as Israel's calling to mission, also help to correct others (Cohen 1982:65).

It was under the Pharisees and scribes that "the faith of Israel became cosmopolitan" (Cohen 1982:57) and by the end of the first century many had converted to Judaism. But the Jews themselves numbered almost 10 % of the world population in that time, while at least a million lived in Egypt and over two million in Judea and Galilee. An additional large number of "God fearers" was on the way to becoming proselytes so adding together all Jews and proselytes they easily came up to the 10 % of the world's population during the days of early Christianity. Among the Pharisees there was the hope that eventually the whole known world would become part of the Jewish faith in the process of Jewish mission. As a number of elements in early Christianity come from Pharisaic Judaism, we can see the Pharisaic drive, for example, in Paul to eventually reach this vision (Cohen 1982:57-58). A number of German New Testament scholars recognise this important mission work of early Judaism starting before the mission of the early church. Scholars such as Jeremias and Hahn are among those who also perceive mission strategies of the early church to be derived from the early Jewish mission work.

Beside this quite optimistic evaluation of Jewish mission in the Roman world, there are other voices who question such strategic mission involvement of Jews altogether. For McKnight, for instance, who understands missionaries to be those who travel with the purpose of evangelism, as Paul did, the Jews were not a missionary movement: "for the Jews of this time, they were a light among the nations, not a light to the nations" (McKnight 2000:842). He argues that even if we can point out a few people who are recognized as travelling evangelists, their first occupancy was not mission but everyday work to earn a living, while New Testament missionaries, such as Paul, were primarily on the road as apostles and not tentmakers (ibid.). As both positions have strong arguments in their favour, we may need to postpone the final word and expect some solutions from future scholarship while recognizing that the New Testament frequently mentions proselytes and God-fearers as a result of witness in the Diaspora. It was the initiative of Hellenistic Jewish Christians that really triggered the mission of the early church (Schnabel 2002:1477-1478).

With the Christ event we again find the double understanding of mission, with emphasis on the one that directs its efforts toward the nations. However, before this could happen, messengers were sent to the Jews. In the Acts of the Apostles we find a clear differentiation between the Jewish people and the religious and political establishment. The leadership is opposed to the new movement while the people seem to respect it. Looking through the sermons as key indicators of the positions of the early movement, one realises that all the speeches—those of Peter, Stephen and Paul—call the whole people of Israel to repent. At the same time, following Old Testament prophets, they seem to expect that only a remnant will be saved. There is no difference between salvation of Jews, Samaritans and Gentiles—salvation happens through the Messiah Jesus who is the only way.

Symbolic events underline that during the Pentecost experience something similar happened as in the Exodus when the nation of Israel was formed. Parallels between the old and the new are drawn with 12 apostles and 120 believers in Acts 1, the specific setting of the community in Jerusalem in Acts 2 and further, the holiness of God in Acts 5 beside whom there is no place for sin. In this renewal of Israel it is also expected that the Spirit will bring the Samaritan people back into this one movement. Even the stories of the eunuch and of the household of Cornelius signify the renewal of Israel and the fulfilment of eschatological prophecies about Israel.

Only Barnabas and Paul's direct mission to the Gentiles challenges the model where Israel is at the centre (Seccombe 1998:351ff).
Conflicts arise and a decision is made in Acts 15, which shifts the
dynamics in taking away the central role of Jerusalem even before
the fall of the city. But this sequence of events is integral to the
new movement as a continuation of the Jewish mission to Gentiles. Until the end of Paul's ministry we find parallel efforts, one
for an integrated 'all nations' church model and one for a purely
Jewish church, primarily in Judea and Galilee. At the end of the first
century, the Jewish church model suffers the loss of its centre and
diminishes, while at the same time the integrated model continues
to have a number of large centres.

2.2 Biblical call to witness to the Jews

As we read the Acts of the Apostles, we can certainly say that the
beginnings of the new movement were in Jerusalem at the centre
of Judaism. Acts 1:8 poses the historical Jerusalem if not as the
centre of global Christianity, as early Christians had hoped, then at
least as the starting point, the birthplace of a new Messianic movement. Right from the beginning the Pentecost event is presented as
a global event and people from different parts of the known world
are present. Jerusalem remained the centre of Christian witness at
least up to Acts 15. Robert Wall argues that Acts 2:22-15:12 "is a
narrative commentary on Joel 3:1-5 (Acts 2:17-21)" (1998:443) and
a fulfilment of promises to the Jews, and that "Acts 15:13-28:28
[needs to be read] as a narrative commentary on Amos 9:11-12 (Acts
15:16-17)" (ibid., 449). If this is true, then at no point does either
of the Old Testament texts talk about a rejection of Israel, as do
some Christians. For instance Pesch, who does not perceive in Acts
28:11-28 yet another attempt of Paul to witness to Jews about their
Messiah, but considers this to be the final scene of a two-volume
piece that terminates the mission to Jews. For him the end of Acts
is the last point where the early Christian mission definitely turns
to Gentiles, a mission with a message that is welcomed by Gentiles
without posing those obstacles as experienced in the early witness
to the Jews (Pesch 2, 1986:306).

One can affirm that the road of witnessing to Jews clearly started in Jerusalem and leads up to Rome. But is Rome the final point where mission to Jews is dismissed? Is there still a call to witness to Jews, or is there no further hope? Or is there possibly a different road of salvation for Jews rather than through Jesus Christ? This so very important that the final part of Acts, the ending of the narrative theology of Luke, needs to receive deeper analysis and scrutiny, as it has been interpreted as the end of mission to the Jews throughout church history.

When Luke finishes his second volume, we realise that he, in fact, has not answered two major questions, as Marshall underlines (1980:420): what has happened with Paul's court case and how does the church in Rome relate to Paul? The canon includes Paul's letter with a deep interest in a church in Rome that already existed at that time. However, Luke writes only about Paul's meeting with non-believing Jews. This is most surprising. Also, it appears somewhat strange, if Acts 1:8 is to be a content statement of Luke's second volume and Rome stands as the 'ends of the earth' to which the Gospel should be taken (Williams 1993:450), that it ends exactly where it had started in Acts 2: with witnessing to non-believing Jews first of all. Does such a development possibly point to the continuing need for witness to Jews as a way to witness to the world? Can this text be interpreted at all as a proposal to leave the mission to Jews and witness only to other nations?

It is interesting to recognise, together with Haenchen, that Paul invests a whole day in order to convince non-believing Jews in Rome of the Gospel, that is now described as the "kingdom of God". At the end of the book, and probably at the end of his life, and after all his negative experiences in witnessing to Jews, Paul is full of passion for the Jews (Haenchen 1959: 646-647). But the non-believing Jews end up in a disagreement, and Luke presents two parties both of whom do not believe in Christ in a full sense (v. 24) and none of them takes the position to become a follower of Christ (Haenchen 1959:647). This seems even more evident by the reaction of Paul and his last words in Acts. Schnabel believes he detects some conversions from among this Jewish group (2002:1212), which is not quite evident from the text.

Paul recognises that the words he quotes from Isaiah 6 were sayings about a past generation. Echoes of this quotation can be heard in words spoken by Jesus in the Gospels, in the Epistle to the Romans written by Paul and once again we see them appear in this narrative. The Jews seem not to be able to realise that God is acting on their behalf and inviting them to himself through his Messiah, Jesus, and his ambassador, Paul.[24] That this same Gospel would be listened to and believed by Gentiles, seems to be paralleled by Rom. 11:11, as Williams (1993: 453.454) rightly points out, with the same goal of provoking Jews to "jealousy" in order that, as in Rom. 11:26, "all Israel would be saved".

The short epilogue at the end of the book of Acts (Acts 28:30-31) can possibly be understood in this way as for two years Paul continues a ministry among Gentiles, as Pesch interprets it (Pesch 2, 1986:311). A careful reading of Acts also allows a different interpretation, because one constantly observes that whenever Paul said he would focus on Gentiles, he still continued to work with both Jews and Gentiles (see, for example, his work in Corinth or Ephesus), building up church communities of Jewish and Gentile Christians along the model of Antioch. Reading this passage in light of Romans 9-11 clearly means that the command to witness to the ends of the earth, according to Acts 1:8, maintains validity for all nations, without a limitation to Jews only but certainly also including the Jewish people and pointing out for them the same way of salvation as is available to other nations. As explicated in Rom. 11:25-32, a "change of heart on their part" is expected of Jews as a chosen nation (Marshall 1980:425) in order to be corporately saved. Fisher (1982:14-15) sounds a helpful caution for the church's reading of the text in Acts: "The New Testament authors take a variety of stances on Jews and Judaism, many negative and polemic in the inflated rhetoric that was the style of the day. But this was as Jews speaking to fellow Jews, not as 'outsiders' condemning Israel in absolute fashion, as the Gentile Church would soon learn to do over the course of the next few centuries. The major question facing the early Church was whether or not Gentiles could be included in the Christian community".

With the epilogue Luke indicates the possibility of continuation, and possibly he hoped, as Marshall (1980:425) believes, to write a third volume before the "pogrom" of Christians in Rome under Nero, which probably led to Paul's execution. But, as argued above, we have no evidence, even with the ending with which Luke leaves the Acts of the Apostles, that there is no continuing mission toward the Jews, as some still try to read into the text of Acts (Senior/ Stuhlmueller 1984:272). The Jewish mission continued (Goldberg 2003:14-23), but at the same time the Christian church grew more rapidly through Gentiles and refocused itself. It probably experienced this paradigm shift shortly after the destruction of Jerusalem, a paradigm shift from predominantly Jewish to Hellenistic Christianity, and left many Messiah believing Jews behind while shaping its Hellenistic Christian doctrines. Throughout the centuries it developed its doctrines and dogmas during church councils that excluded the Jewishness of the Gospel and partly the Jewish Christ (Bosch 1991: 55-57, Goldberg 2003:17-18).

2.3 Messianic Jews and Messianic Mission

The recent rise of the Messianic movement is possibly the fulfilment of the New Testament concept that Jews as followers of the Messiah would be recognised as an ethnic community. Paul was, till his death, still hoping that Israel would recognise its Messiah (Rom 9-11). James waited in Jerusalem for a corporate turning of the Jews and died without seeing the fulfilment of the Acts 2 hope (see Josephus' comments in *Antiquities* 20, 9). However, we may too quickly follow some evangelical enthusiasm if we say this is how this movement should be interpreted. According to Eckhard J. Schnabel, at the end of the first century about half a million of the world's population in at least 200 different cities believed in Jesus as Messiah and Lord (Schnabel 2002: 1464-1468). Acts provides some hints that at least one fifth of this group must have been ethnic Jews, as at most places where a local church was started it was linked to the Jewish population and often connected to a synagogue. Today we are in a situation similar to the first century in that ethnic Jews are interested in going back to their roots and often this interest includes turning to the Messiah Yeshua. It is again the effort of Jewish believers in the Messiah in which such developments take place, however we evaluate them theologically. As in the early days, they have been the best witnesses for their fellow country people.

On the side of the Christian church we need to recognise the schism of the past, when Gentile Christianity separated itself from Judaism followed by the development of Christian arrogance. Our role is to allow Messianic Jews to develop, as Hellenistic Christianity was allowed to develop in its Hellenistic ways after the Jerusalem Council, recognising that all councils and decisions after the separation between Hellenistic and Jewish Christianity, the first and major schism, have a relative role, and no final authority. If we can do this, we will see a Messianic Judaism develop that is both partly contextualised and yet still needing more space to be relevant in its context.

3. Résumé

A discussion on Judaism and Islam in relation to Christianity has many intricacies, and very easily one can find oneself under suspicion of syncretism, or at least of leaving the orthodox Christian faith as defined by the councils to which all Christian traditions of historic and free churches subscribe. The Jewish Messianic movement is already under suspicion of falling short of explicitly following council decisions and formulations, especially in the area of high christology. Personally, I find myself in a tension of clearly subscribing to the council creeds formulated in the first millennium and, at the same time, supporting the Jewish Messianic movement as well as attempts at deeper contextualisation of Christianity in a Muslim context. How does the New Testament and especially Acts 15 relate to this tension? Analysing Acts 15, we recognise the impressiveness of the step that Messianic Judaism took at the Jerusalem Council toward Hellenistic Christianity in deciding to keep and allow both religious expressions and practices. The early church boldly stepped out of a safe definition of faith and allowed non-Jews to become followers of Jesus without first becoming proselytes of Judaism. We today hesitate to take such a step and, instead, expect groups outside of the Constantinian Christian worldview to become its proselytes in order to become acceptable Christians. This is the main reason why Jews and Arabs frequently do not respond to this kind of a Gospel.

Before we attempt to draw the parallels between then and now with the similarities between Acts 15 and the 21st century, I would like to refer to a table that explains a contextualisation scale of C1—C6 and which missiologists have applied to different cultures and contexts. I am following John Travis and others in their model that is widely used in defining "Christ centred communities in a Muslim context" (Travis 1998: 407-408). Similar attempts at contextualisation have been applied with some positive outcomes in the Messianic Jewish movement. Some testing also goes on today in Arabic contexts and the results usually point out that more openness to contextualisation is required than we often demonstrate.

Such contextualisation needs to be handled with all possible caution in order to remain in line with the Gospel according to the scriptures as it is presented in a Semitic context. This would serve both the Messianic Jewish and Messianic Arab witness. Contextualisation needs to happen not only in a general way but to be specific to each context, so that the Gospel is really spoken in a language that Muslims and Jews understand. One needs to clearly recognise the cultural diversity inside of Jewish and Palestinian contexts, as well as perceive differences between the Sunni, Shiite and Druze Muslim context, and similarly between the various groups of a Jewish context. For our study the specific Palestinian/Israeli context is of importance. A clear understanding of the context will also help us to biblically refocus our own Christian identity (Masri 2005:36).

I will attempt to collect some aspects of suggested contextualisation on the levels C4 to C6 for the Jewish and Arab context and compare them in parallel to European Christianity.[25] Let us identify the contextualisation for the three groups on C4 level (*see Tab. 1*).

C5 goes one step further toward contextualisation and socialisation (*see Tab. 2*).

	Community praxis (C4)	Identity (C4)	View from a wider community (C4)
Muslim Context	Using some "Islamic cultural elements (e.g., dress, music, diet, arts)" that are in line with biblical texts	"Follower of Isa"	A kind of Christian
Jewish Context	Using some Jewish cultural elements that are in line with the New Testament and the Hebrew Bible	Messianic/ Christian Jew	A group inside of Christianity and Judaism
European Context	Using cultural elements defined by the Greco-Roman world as interpreted today in line with the biblical texts.	Christian	Active Christians in a wider Christian culture of Europe

Table 14.1: *C4 type community.*

	Community praxis (C5)	Identity (C5)	View from a wider community (C5)
Muslim Context	Similar to C4, but the person is much more integrated in their Muslim surroundings and maintains a tension between the faiths	"Muslim follower of Jesus"	A distinct kind of Muslim
Jewish Context	Follows all Jewish customs, feasts, regularly visits the synagogue	Messianic Jew	A distinct kind of Jew
European Context	Integrates former heathen feasts (Easter, Christmas, etc.) and customs into the Christian faith	Traditional Christian	A group developed inside which is part of Constantinian Christendom

Table 14.2: *C5 type community.*

	Community praxis (C6)	Identity (C6)	View from a wider community (C6)
Muslim Context	Secret believers who may or may not be active members in the religious life of the Muslim community	Privately believing in Isa	Religious but not actively involved in any kind of faith community
Jewish Context	Secret believer in Yeshua but not connected to any kind of Christian community	Privately believing in Yeshua	Involved in Jewish praxis as expected by society
European Context	Passive believer in the Christian God, sometimes visiting Christian gatherings but not on a regular basis	Private, individual Christian	Personal piety, but not active in community

Table 14.3: *C6 type community.*

One further step, that some will possibly define as being outside of the Christian faith and rarely consider its members as Christians, can be seen in C6. Groups contextualising the Gospel on this level would not be part of a visible community confessing Jesus as Christ/ Messiah. The issues of contextualisation rather become issues of an individual believer and the way how he/she expresses faith (*see Tab. 3*).

Most Christians and their witnessing activities to Jews and Palestinian Muslims will still find themselves in C1 to C3 (Travis 1998:407-408):

C1:A church foreign to the community in culture and language

C2: Similar to C1, but the church partly accepts the language of the community and translates its concepts into the language of the community while still maintaining traditional concepts of explaining Christian faith (Constantinian Christianity). Terminology and cultural expressions are distinct from the community's context.

C3: Still maintains worship elements, dress, diet, and other expressions of faith that are foreign to the community's praxis.

It is this kind of Christian witness that has been primarily rejected as arrogant and proselytising. A Christian missionary believes he/ she is bringing Christ along with him/herself, instead of recognising that Christ is already there and can be recognised in the Jewish and Muslim faith. From this recognition and type of understanding people can be guided to experiencing and following the biblical Messiah.

This paper, in some aspects still quite fragile and maybe even contradictory, is a call for new contextualisation efforts on behalf of religious Jews and Palestinian Muslims, that we find only partly applied today but that need more consideration and development. The Semitic reading of the Gospel by Messianic Jews may be a doorway for Messianic Muslims in the 21st century that can possibly open the way for a renewal both in religious Judaism and in Palestinian Muslim contexts. This renewal will not come from outside and will not draw believers in Jesus Christ out of their families and communities. Instead, as in the Messianic Jewish movement, Messianic Muslims would be those who reach out to their brothers and sisters and together unite in true worship that is not focused on Mecca or Jerusalem, but is focused on the God who has sent his Messiah and his Spirit to gather people to himself.

As in New Testament times, the Father can use the Christ and the Spirit not only to draw Jews and Palestinians to himself but at the same time to draw them to each other for reconciliation. As God was able in Christ and through the Spirit to overcome the gap and the wall between Jews and Samaritans as well as between Jews and Gentiles, he can overcome the schism between Jews, Muslims and Christians in the Holy Land and beyond. Biblical contextualisation of the Gospel, as modelled in Acts and the whole of the Scripture, is the way we need to go while dropping those dogmas that were relevant for contextualisation in the past but that in the present time divide instead of unite Christians. Recognising the past history and the theology of each of the groups—Jews, Muslims and Christians,— it is important to follow the call that we hear throughout history, as in the time of the Reformation in Europe, the call back to the sources that would help us to reinterpret the past and present, to be relevant and biblical for the presence and future. The Gospel of God's salvation, as presented in the New Testament and reinterpreted in different local contexts, will allow people of different cultural and religious backgrounds to find inside and sometimes also against, their community the way to God's heart. Mistakes are inevitable on this way as are tensions. These mistakes can be forgiven as long as all of this happens in the Spirit of the Messiah Jesus, as proclaimed according to the New Testament in the world, in love, reconciliation and peace.

Endnotes

1   The recent book by Jimmy Carter on *Palestine: Peace not Apartheid* starts with the Abrahamic story that is tied to the "Holy Land" and shows that it is impossible to separate current issues and the role that this land plays for all three Abrahamic faiths.

2   See, for example, the strong statements by Kremers (1979:7-27) who cannot see any legitimate Christian mission to the Jews. For the Catholic church, a document published in 1991 *Dialogue and Proclamation* summarises that dialogue is preferred instead of attempts to convert persons from their faith to one's own religion. However, dialogue should encourage "a deeper conversion of all toward God" and does not exclude that in the "process of conversion (to God) the decision may be made to leave one's own previous spiritual or religious situation in order to direct oneself toward another" (Hinze and Omar 2005:63).

3   It seems that, according to the Gospels, Jesus has also been somewhat hesitant to use the term Messiah for himself, possibly for the reason that he was not planning to fulfil expectations placed in Judaism, at that time and up to the present, upon the Messiah, especially in relation to some nationalistic and militant ideas. On the other hand, the use of the term Messiah in New Testament texts demonstrates that he was perceived as the expected Messiah of the Jews [John 1:41]: The first thing Andrew did was to find his brother Simon and tell him, "We have found the *Messiah*" (that is, the Christ). He is also the Messiah for the Samaritans [John 4:25.26]: The woman said, "I know that *Messiah* (called Christ) is coming. When he comes, he will explain everything to us." Then Jesus declared, "I who speak to you am he." He is clearly the Christ of all. The texts also show that some of the expectations in Judaism needed to be refocused following the Hebrew Bible against later traditions of Judaism (Ps. Sol. 17:22-25; 4 Esd 13:8-10; 2 Bar 38-40; and other later Jewish literature). In his Pentecost sermon, the Apostle Peter clearly points to Jesus as Messiah (Acts 2:36).

4   Lisa Loden, in her paper "Messianic Jewish Views of Israel's Rebirth and Survival in the Light of Scripture" at the November conference in Prague 2006.

5   Philipp Saa'd, in his presentation "How Shall We Interpret Scripture about the Land and Eschatology? Jewish and Arab Perspectives" at the November conference in Prague 2006.

6   The discussion about a Constantinian replacement theology in contrast to dispensational theology continues in evangelical Christianity. It seems that both positions recognise some truths but miss the biblical view, as they press the text into their system. (Sholocha 2007:7-50). After all, we expect Christ to come again not in Rome, Wittenberg,

Moscow or L.A., but in Jerusalem. This underlines that there is still some role for this city and the peoples (Jews, Muslims and Christians) who live in this city.

7 This discussion is primarily western and is not found in the Arab world. Christine Schirrmacher in her book (2001) stands for such a position that the God of Qur'an is not the Christian God. In her chapter on "Koran and Bible Compared" she clearly argues that Allah is different from the God of the New Testament. This may be quite obvious especially when we discuss the issue of Trinity. But in the issue of Trinity Christianity also differs from Judaism as monotheism in the New Testament is redefined but maintains that God is one. Looking at the character of the Christian God, as Schirrmacher does (2001:12-17), we will clearly identify differences from the God of Islam but also from the God of the Jews. To abandon the word Allah for God because of these considerations may lead us to what Marcion did with the Old Testament, defining his canon and avoiding the Old Testament God. As Christian theologians we would not do this. At the same time we avoid historical information about Allah in Islam. The name Allah was used by Arab Christians for the God of our Lord Jesus even before the Qur'an was written. In Christian apologetic there is discussion about what religion worships God most appropriately but not whether Christians and Muslims worship the same God (cf. Griffith 2002). Tragically, there was no full Bible translation into Arabic during the time of Mohammad while the other nations in the region had the biblical texts in their own language. Some see in this the reason for the need of a book in Arabic, the book of Qur'an. But in Christian poetry and some shorter translations of the New Testament in Arabic one finds Allah as the name for the God of the Bible. See also Arabic-language manuscripts at Houghton Library: Guide (January 9, 2007)http://oasis.harvard.edu:10080/oasis/deliver/~hou01854. It is more problematic when the word Allah is used outside of Arabic and would sound as strange in other languages as if we would use the English word God in the Arabic language (www.submission.org/allah-god.html). The use of Allah in the Qur'an may have had a strong influence on Mohammad in his understanding of who God is, especially through Christianity but also through Mohammad's interaction with Judaism (articles by George Khoury: http://www.ewtn.com/library/chistory/eveislam.htm; http://www.al-bushra.org/arbhrtg/arbxtn01.htm - Arabic Christian Literature; http://www.al-bushra.org/mag08/earbxt.htm - Arab Christian Literature of the 8th-9th centuries). The development of Islam can be easily viewed as an imitation of and at the same time a reaction against the Constantinian Christendom and the Judaism of those days, contextualised into the Arab world as Christianity was contextualised in the Hellenistic and Latin world. Mohammad himself was part of the Arab Christian movement so that we could, in fact, speak of a schism that lead to Arab Islam and Constantinian Christianity. This

does not make Muslims evangelical Christians in the same way as Jews are not evangelicals, but it makes them a family to which we as evangelicals belong, even as we share the Christian redefined monotheism as we find it in the Christian Bible that differs from Jews and Muslims. But it is the same Abrahamic God in whom we believe.

8 We recognise that, latest in Antioch, we find persons of non-Jewish origins joining early Christianity, the people of God.

9 At the Arab Baptist Theological Seminary in Beirut, Lebanon, and especially at their Institute of Islamic Studies we can find some fresh thinking on Arab Muslims and how to witness, relate to and experience them as people by destroying walls that have been developed through hate and prejudice. Key people in this positive approach toward Arab Muslims are Martin Accad, Nizar Masri and others.

10 Williamson argues that we need to differentiate between this resettled group and the Samaritans that we find in the New Testament (1992:726).

11 Some question the relatedness of the Samaritans who lived during Jesus' time to those who are mentioned in the earlier Hebrew texts, even including Ezra's comments. Some, following Josephus' comments, expect that the Samaritans were a priestly group that had left the Jerusalem priesthood after being hindered at reform attempts. So they perceive a certain parallel to the Qumran community. But there are not enough sources to argue this or the opposite position.

12 Moses figures prominently in the Samaritan faith, but this way they also identify with the patriarchs and Abraham.

13 It is astonishing to realise that Ishmael, other than the promise of land, receives almost the same blessings as Isaac.

14 We may compare Muhammad with an Old Testament prophet such as Amos to see what similar roles both have in the different nations.

15 There are discussions among scholars that Samaritan beliefs were, in fact, more significant during the time of the New Testament and that their influence on the New Testament and on the early church development has been underestimated (Anderson and Giles 2002:40-42). Recent debates about Stephen of Acts 6 and 7 try to perceive him as a Samaritan believer, rather than a Hellenistic Jew. The theology that is expressed and quotes used in the speech of Stephen point to the Samaritans and their Pentateuch. Others see in Hebrews 9:3–4 evidence of a Samaritan text and reading (Anderson 2000:1054). This opens for us a much wider horizon as we think of Samaritans and their influence in the early church.

16 Scroggs (1999:69-91) clearly works with this assumption when presenting the social setting of the early Christian community emerging with its sectarian characteristics.

17 Stephen raises questions similar to the ones that Samaritans had about the Temple, in God's view of the Temple (7:42-50), but we find similar positions also in the Qumran community (cf. Keener 1993:342). Also, the text goes well with the LXX. "[I]t has also been suggested that behind the speech of Stephen in Acts 7 lies a Samaritan theology and that Stephen was either a Samaritan and not a Hellenist (Spiro) or that the Hellenists were markedly influenced by Samaritan theology (Scobie)" (Maynard-Reid 1997:1076)

18 Justin the Martyr refers to him as the one who plays an important role in spreading Gnostic ideas (*Apology*, 1.26). Yamauchi summarises the Church Father's view on "Simon of Samaria as the arch-Gnostic" whose disciples have continued to impart Gnostic influences throughout the Roman Empire (2000:414). Anderson introduces another very interesting aspect about Simon and Gnosticism: "Simon Magus (Acts 8:9–24) and Melchizedek (an important focus of Hebrews) may tie together Gnosticism, Christianity and the Samaritans. That Simon was a Samaritan is implied by the fourteenth-century Samaritan Chronicler Abu'l Fath and by the early church fathers who also identified him as a Gnostic, though both labels are still debated. Simon and Stephen represent diametrically opposed expressions of Samaritan Christianity— Gnostic versus historical Christianity" (2000:414-415).

19 Pelikan (2005:110) rightfully notices that when Simon desires to have the power to pass on the Holy Spirit he, in fact, desires to purchase a church office for money, which frequently happened in the past and may still happen in the present. But the ministry of an apostle is not passed on to others; it is Christ's prerogative to appoint people to different ministries in the church, as Paul clearly defines in Eph. 4:11.

20 Mark S. Kinzer deals in his book with the difficult relations of Christian mission to the Jews. See also Martin A. Cohen and Helga Croner (1982) and H. Kremers (1979).

21 Goldberg believes in 2003 that there were "more than three hundred Messianic congregations in the United States, while some ninety Messianic congregations exist in Israel" (2003:25). The survey conducted in 1999 by Kjaer-Hansen and Skjott (now somewhat dated) analysed 81 congregations in Israel. Many of them showed enormous growth between the early 90s and the time of the survey due to new immigrants from Eastern Europe and those of the new immigrants who have come to faith while already in Israel (1999:38-39, 49-52).

22 See, for example, Louis Goldberg, ed. *How Jewish is Christianity; Facts and Myths about the Messianic Congregations in Israel*; Carol

Harris-Shapiro, *Messianic Judaism*. Beacon Press, 1999; Dan Cohn-Sherbok, *Messianic Judaism*. Cassell, 2000; Jeffrey Wasserman, *Messianic Congregations*. University Press of America, 2000.

23 An excellent book from within the Messianic Jewish and Christian Palestinian debate presenting views of Christian Arabs, Messianic Jews and Western Christians is *The Bible and the Land: An Encounter,* edited by Lisa Loden, Peter Walker and Michael Wood. A more pro-Palestinian perspective can be found in the book *Justice, and only Justice—A Palestinian Theology of Liberation* by Naim Stivan Ateek, a perspective that is usually little known in the West.

24 It is important to recognise that the text in Acts where Paul quotes from Is. 6: 9,10 seems to point to Ez. 2:3-5 and 3:4-7, as Schnabel rightly indicates. This brings out even more the notion that Paul attempted to provoke the Jews to respond positively to Jesus as Messiah rather than, as often understood, that he believes God has rejected Israel. This would also fit with Paul's future involvement in continuing to witness to both, Jews and Gentiles, as he did in the past (Schnabel 2002:1212).

25 I am using here Nizar Masri's suggestions on contextualisation in a Muslim context from a table in his dissertation on "The Prospects and Challenges of a Messianic Movement within the Context of Arab-Islam" (34). I have adapted the table to include parallels to European and Jewish Christianity.

References

Anderson, Robert T. and Terry Giles. *The Keepers: an Introduction to the History and Culture of the Samaritans.* Peabody: Hendrickson, 2002.

Anderson, Robert T. and Terry Giles. *Tradition Kept: the Literature of the Samaritans.* Peabody: Hendrickson, 2005.

Anderson, Robert T. "Samaritan Literature," in: *Dictionary of New Testament Background,* ed. by Craig A. Evans and Stanley E. Porter. Downers Grove: InterVarsity Press, 2000.

Ateek, Naim Stivan. *Justice, and only Justice—A Palestinian Theology of Liberation.* Maryknoll: Orbis books, 1990.

Bevans, B. Stephen. *Models of Contextual Theology: Faith and Cultures.* Maryknoll: Orbis books, 2002.

Boers, Hendrikus. *Neither on this Mountain nor in Jerusalem.* Scholars Press, 1988.

Bosch, David J. *Transforming Mission—Paradigm Shifts in Theology of Mission*. Maryknoll: Orbis books, 1991.

Carter, Jimmy. *Palestine Peace not Apartheid*. New York: Simon & Schuster, 2006.

Cohen, Martin A. "The Mission of Israel: A Theologico-Historical Analysis," in: *Christian Mission-Jewish Mission, Studies in Judaism and Christianity*, ed. by Martin A. Cohen and Helga Croner. A Stimulus Book. Ramsey: Paulist Press, 1982:46-79.

Cohen, Martin A. and Helga Croner, eds. *Christian Mission - Jewish Mission, Studies in Judaism and Christianity*. A Stimulus Book. Ramsey: Paulist Press, 1982.

Fisher, Eugene J. "Historical Developments in the Theology of Christian Mission," in: *Christian Mission-Jewish Mission, Studies in Judaism and Christianity*, ed. by Martin A. Cohen and Helga Croner. A Stimulus Book. Ramsey: Paulist Press, 1982:4-45.

Goldberg, Louis. *How Jewish is Christianity? Two Views on the Messianic Movement*. Grand Rapids: Zondervan, 2003.

Griffith, Sidney H. *The Beginnings of Christian theology in Arabic: Muslim-Christian encounters in the early Islamic Period*. Ashgate, 2002.

Haenchen, Ernst. *Die Apostelgeschichte*. KEK Göttingen. Vandenhoeck & Ruprecht, 1959.

Harnack, von Adolph. *The Mission and Expansion of Christianity in the First Three Centuries*. Gloucester: Peter Smith, 1972 [1908].

Hinze, Bradford R. and Irfan A. Omar, eds. *Heirs of Abraham: the Future of Muslim, Jewish and Christian Relations*. Maryknoll: Orbis, 2005.

Josephus, Flavius. "Antiquities of the Jews," in *The Works of Flavius Josephus*, tr. by William Whiston. Boston: D. Lothrop Company, 1886.

Justin the Martyr, "The First Apology," in *The Fathers of the Church*, ed. by Ludwig Schopp. New York: Christian Heritage, 1048.

Keener, Craig S. *Bible Background Commentary of the New Testament*. Downers Grove: InterVarsity Press, 1993.

Kinzer, Mark S. *Post-Missionary Messianic Judaism: redefining Christian engagement with the Jewish people*. Grand Rapids: Brazos, 2005.

Kjaer-Hansen, Kai and Bodil F. Skjott. *Facts and Myths about the Messianic Congregations in Israel*. Jerusalem: Caspari Center, 1999.

Kremers, Heinz. *Judenmission heute?* Neukirchen-Vluyn: Neukirchener Verlag, 1979.

Loden, Lisa, Peter Walker and Michael Wood, eds. *The Bible and the Land: An Encounter, Different Views: Christian Arab Palestinian, Israeli Messianic Jew, Western Christian.* Jerusalem: Musalaha, 2000.

Longenecker, Richard N. *The Acts of the Apostles. The Expositor's Bile Commentary, vol. 9.* Ed. by Frank E. Gaebelein. Regency Reference Library. Grand Rapids: Zondervan, 1981.

Marshall, I. Howard. *Acts.* Tyndale New Testament Commentaries. Grand Rapids: Eerdmans, 1980.

Masri, Nizar. The Prospects and Challenges of a Messianic Movement within the Context of Arab-Islam. Unpublished MTh. Dissertation. IBTS/University of Wales, June 2006.

Maynard-Reid, P. U. "Samaria," in: *Dictionary of the Later New Testament & its Developments,* ed. by Ralph P. Martin and Peter H. Davids. Downers Grove: InterVarsity Press, 1997: 1075-1077.

McKnight, S. "Proselytism and Godfearers," in: *Dictionary of New Testament Background,* ed. by Craig A. Evans and Stanley E. Porter. Downers Grove: InterVarsity Press, 2000: 835-847.

Morris, Leon. *The Gospel According to John.* The New International Commentary on the New Testament. Grand Rapids: Eerdmans, 1971.

Pelikan, Jeroslav. *Acts.* Brazos Theological Commentary on the Bible. Brazos Press, 2005.

Pesch, Rudolf. *Die Apostelgeschichte (Apg 13-28).* Evangelisch-Katholischer Kommentar zum Neuen Testament Bd. V/2. Neukirchen-Vluyn: Neukirchener Verlag, 1986.

Pesch, Rudolf. *Die Apostelgeschichte (Apg 1-12.)* Evangelisch-Katholischer Kommentar zum Neuen Testament Bd. V/1. Neukirchen-Vluyn: Neukirchener Verlag, 1986.

Robinson, Rich. "Jewish Missions," in: *Evangelical Dictionary of World Missions,* ed. by A. Scott Moreau. Cumbria: Paternoster Press, 2000: 521-522.

Schirrmacher, Christine. *The Islamic View on Major Christian Teachings: The role of Jesus Christ, Sin, Faith and Forgiveness.* Hamburg: Reformatorischer Verlag Beese, 2001.

Schnabel, Eckard J. *Urchristliche Mission.* TVG. R. Brockhaus: Wuppertal, 2002.

Schnackenburg, Rudolf. *Das Johannesevangelium,* Teil 1: Einleitung und Kommentar zu 1-4. Freiburg: Herder Publishing, 1965.

Schneider, Johannes. *Das Evangelium nach Johannes*, Sonderband in: Theologischer Handkommentar zum Neuen Testament. Berlin: Evangelische Verlagsanstalt, ⁴1988.

Schreiter, J. Robert. *Constructing Local Theologies*. With a forward by Edward Schillebeeckx. Maryknoll: Orbis Books, 1985.

Scroggs, Robin. "The Earliest Christian Communities as Sectarian Movement," in: David G. Horrell (ed), *Social-Scientific Approaches to New Testament Interpretation*. T & T Clark, 1999.

Seccombe, David. "The New People of God" in: *Witness to the Gospel—The Theology of Acts*. I. Howard Marshall and David Peterson (eds), Eerdmans, 1998.

Senior, Donald and Carroll Stuhlmueller, *The Biblical Foundations for Mission*. Maryknoll: Orbis Press, 1984.

Sholocha, Sergey. "Prophecies of Israel's Future—The Hermeneutics of Covenant Theology and Dispensationalism." *Theological Reflections* 7 (2007): 7-50 (in Russian and English language).

Solomon, Norman, Richard Harries and Tim Winter. *Abraham's Children: Jews, Christians and Muslims in Conversation*. London: T&T Clarl, 2005.

Tenney, Merrill C. *The Gospel of John*. The Expositor's Bible Commentary, vol. 9, ed. by Frank E. Gaebelein. Regency Reference Library. Grand Rapids: Zondervan, 1981.

Travis, John. "The C1 to C6 Spectrum: A Practical Tool for Defining Six Types of 'Christ-centered Communities' (C) Found in the Muslim Context." *Evangelical Missions Quarterly* 34 (October 1998): 407-408.

Travis, John. "Messianic Muslim Followers of Isa: A Closer Look at C5 Believers and Congregations." *International Journal of Frontier Missions* 17 (Spring 2000): 53-59.

Wall, Robert. "Israel and the Gentile Mission in Acts and Paul: A Canonical Approach" in: *Witness to the Gospel—The Theology of Acts,* I. Howard Marshall and David Peterson (eds). Grand Rapids: Eerdmans, 1998, 437-457.

Williams, David J. *Acts*. New International Biblical Commentary. Peabody: Hendrickson Publishing, 1993.

Williamson H. G. M. and C. A. Evans. "Samaritans" in: *Dictionary of New Testament Background*, Craig A. Evens and Stanley E. Porter (eds). Downers Grove: Inter Varsity Press, 2000: 1056-1061.

Zangenberg, Jürgen. *Frühes Christentum in Samarien: topographische und traditionsgeschichtliche Studien zu den Samarientexten im Johannesevangelium*. Marburg: Francke Verlag, 1998.

Yamauchi E. M., "Gnosticism", in: *Dictionary of New Testament Background*, Craig A. Evens and Stanley E. Porter (eds). Downers Grove: Inter Varsity Press, 2000: 414-418.

Yee, Tet-Lim N. *Jews, Gentiles and Ethnic Reconciliation: Paul's Jewish Identity and Ephesians*. Society for New Testament Studies (Monograph Series). Cambridge: Cambridge University Press, 2005.

15

Jesus and Just Peacemaking Theory

GLEN STASSEN

Until recently we have had only two paradigms in Christian ethics for questions of war and violence: pacifism and just war theory. They focus discussion on the question: Should we make this war or not?

But this diverts us from discussing the equally important question: What actions should we be taking to prevent war?

It's like only discussing whether divorce should be allowed, and never discussing what actions husbands, wives, and churches should be taking to make marriages more peaceful and more fulfilling, and prevent divorce.

Now we have a third paradigm in Christian ethics—Just Peacemaking Theory.[1] It points to the peacemaking practices that Jesus taught and that actually work to make peace and prevent war. It focuses discussion on actions of healing and prevention.

During World War II, my father experienced fierce battles with the Japanese Navy in the South Pacific. He then saw the devastation in Japan itself. Even before the Japanese surrender was signed, he and three other sailors rushed in a jeep to a total of fourteen Japanese Prisoner of War camps, rescuing prisoners. When he got home, he showed us photos of emaciated and starving prisoners. He had also seen the devastation of Tokyo from the fire bombing. He told me: "War is so terrible that we have to do all we can to prevent

World War III. And we have to do all we can to prevent war with atomic bombs."

Later, when I was a teenager, during the years of the Cold War and hostility between the United States and the Soviet Union, my pastor, V. Carney Hargroves, made trips to Baptist churches in Russia with a message of peace, and he invited a pastor of the Moscow Baptist Church to come preach in our church. When the governments were opposed to peacemaking, my pastor was leading peacemaking in Baptist churches.

One Sunday morning in church, I received a vision. It was a vision that churches would really do the teachings of Jesus and would be a significant influence for the peacemaking that Jesus calls for. I remember that experience vividly; I know exactly where I was sitting—on the left side, about one-third of the way back, near the aisle. I was looking up at the ceiling, and thinking about the church, while my pastor was preaching.

So I went to seminary and graduate school, studied biblical teaching on peacemaking, studied what political scientists have determined actually does work to prevent wars, and wrote a book developing an ethic that focuses on seven initiatives of peacemaking that prevent war.[2]

Soon other teachers of Christian ethics said "this is the kind of ethic that we have needed for a long time." So twenty-three Christian ethicists from different denominations (including four experts in international relations and three leaders of citizens' peacemaking organizations) joined together to develop a just peacemaking ethic that they could agree on despite their differences. It took four years, but we reached unanimous consensus on the ten practices of just peacemaking. We published it as *Just Peacemaking: Ten Practices to Abolish War* (Pilgrim Press, 1998). Each practice has in fact prevented some wars, and the ten together are an effective force for peacemaking. Now we know where to put our shoulders to the wheel, and in which direction to push, in order to prevent many wars and save death and misery for millions of children, women, and men whom God loves. We don't think these peacemaking practices, in obedience to the way of Jesus, will bring in the full kingdom of God, but we think they are mustard seeds of the kingdom that will prevent enormous suffering and misery in war.

Just peacemaking theory also opens up a new perspective on biblical study. Guided by the questions posed by just peacemaking theory, rich new biblical resources are opening up. What did God mean by telling Cain he could do the right thing? Jesus answers it in Matthew 5:23-26: Go, make peace with your brother. What initiatives did Jacob take to make peace with Esau, and what initiatives did Joseph and his brothers take to make peace with each other? What initiatives did the prophets say were the will of God in order to avoid the destruction of war?[3] What peacemaking initiatives did Jesus command? When Paul wrote all his letters as calls to peace based on grace, what kinds of peacemaking initiatives did he urge?

The ten practices of just peacemaking surely can help in working for peace in the Middle East. Let us look at them, one at a time. They come in three clusters: initiatives, justice, and community.

1 Transforming initiatives

1.1 Nonviolent direct action

Matthew 5:38-42 teaches transforming initiatives of nonviolent confrontation. Matthew 5:39 is usually mistranslated "Do not resist evil." This makes no sense: Jesus regularly resisted evil, confronting it directly. As Walter Wink, followed by N.T. Wright, points out, the Greek word translated "resist" means violent and revengeful resistance.[4] And as Clarence Jordan points out, Greek grammar says the word translated "evil" can equally as well be translated as "by evil means." The decision must come from the context. Jesus repeatedly confronts and resists evil. It got him crucified. But he did not practice *evil means*—hate, violence, revenge, domination, or self-righteous exclusion. He rejected violent defense in the Garden. Therefore the context clearly favors "do not resist revengefully by evil means."[5] This translation is confirmed by Romans 12:14-21, where Paul gives us Jesus' teaching as "Never avenge yourselves.... Do not be overcome by evil, but overcome evil by good [means]."

Jesus then gives us the peacemaking practices, the transforming initiatives: turn the other cheek, give both your shirt and your cloak, go the second mile, and give to the one who begs. Analogously, Paul gives two transforming initiatives in Romans 12: feed your hungry enemy, and give a drink to your thirsty enemy. New Testament scholarship is now interpreting these as transforming initiatives—creative ways to confront an adversary's action, include the adversary in community, assert the adversary's dignity, and ask for peacemaking.

For example, Jesus' teaching on the second mile has its meaning in the context of being compelled by a Roman soldier to carry his pack one mile. Jesus does not emphasize what we are *not* to do, such as pull out a knife and kill him, or comply sullenly, breathing resentment all the way. Rather, he emphasizes taking our own transforming initiative, carrying it a *second* mile, and, if it is combined with 5:23ff., making peace while on the way.

Similarly, Jesus' teaching on the left cheek has its context where a person in that shame-and-honor culture is slapped with a demeaning, back-handed slap on the right cheek. Since that culture did not allow touching someone with your left hand, a slap on the right cheek would be a back-handed slap.[6] Turning the left cheek is a nonviolent confrontation of the wrong; it says, "no more backhanded slaps," and asserts dignity, while raising the possibility of peacemaking. Jesus' emphasis is on a nonviolent direct action of confrontation and peacemaking.[7]

Jesus' teaching that you are to give not only your coat but also your cloak also means not only complying with what you are forced to do, but taking a surprising initiative. You would be standing there naked in the law court, revealing the greed of the person suing in all its nakedness.

The structure of the whole central section of the Sermon from 5:21-7:12 strongly supports interpreting Jesus' teachings as transforming initiatives. This trend can be seen in the writings of New Testament scholars Dale Allison, Hans Dieter Betz, David Garland, Donald Hagner, Clarence Jordan, Pinchas Lapide, Ulrich Luz, Walter Wink, N. T. Wright, and in my own writing.

In his *Politics of Jesus*,[8] John Howard Yoder reports two cases of collective nonviolent direct action that were successful in changing

Roman policy toward Israel shortly before and after Jesus' ministry. John Domenic Crossan reports seven nonviolent demonstrations by Jews against Roman policies. "All those demonstrations
were nonviolent, all had very specific objectives, and four out of the
seven achieved those objectives without loss of life."[9] This shows
that transforming initiatives of nonviolent action were not unthink-
able or undoable in Jesus' context. They were what Jesus was calling
for, instead of the violent, revengeful resistance that led to Rome's
destruction of Jerusalem and the Temple in 70 A.D.

Nonviolent direct action has emerged in our time as implementing
transforming initiatives toward an enemy. It includes nonviolent
demonstrations, civil disobedience, strikes and boycotts.

I was in East Germany when the whole society experienced the
turning from dictatorial, oppressive, walled-in communist society
to freedom and human rights. I saw the pictures of Martin Luther
King, Jr., on the walls inside the churches, and saw his writings in
the churches, translated into German so people could study together
how to do nonviolent direct action.

On the first Sunday morning after the wall opened, I preached
in the Baptist church in Bitterfeld, and on Sunday afternoon we
went to the Cathedral where thousands had regularly gathered on
Sunday afternoons to listen to speakers, pray, and prepare for nonviolent direct action. After the service in the Cathedral, we went out
into the town square, where people voiced their concerns on the
open microphone. They concluded by singing "We Shall Overcome"
in English. People had not only studied the methods of nonviolent
direct action; they were singing the songs in English! I was powerfully moved as if by the Holy Spirit, and made my way up onto the
platform. I gave the shortest speech I have ever given: "I was deeply
involved in the U.S. civil rights movement. You have done successfully, against great odds, what we were trying to do. I am deeply,
deeply moved, and deeply grateful for what you have done." I got
the biggest applause I have ever gotten in my life. They had indeed
practiced nonviolent direct action, though walled off from the rest
of the world, and they greatly appreciated having the connection
between their struggle and ours be recognized.

All the actions had to be planned and organized in churches; it was illegal to have meetings anywhere else. The churches prayed regularly that the demonstrations would stay nonviolent on both sides. And the churches produced a book-length manifesto, whose title in English would be *Justice, Peace, and the Preservation of Creation.* Its section on "More Justice in the Democratic Republic of Germany" was the one public document that united the people in the changes they demanded.

A week after the wall had been opened, traveling on the Autobahn, we heard the new leader, Hans Modrow, addressing the parliament. We pulled to the side so we could listen carefully. Modrow announced the implementation of the very reforms the church had demanded! And all this had happened without one single person dying. I wept tears of emotionally overwhelming awe and gratitude.

Nonviolent Direct Action is spreading around the world. It was practiced in Poland and Czechoslovakia, in the Philippines, and throughout Latin America. It is achieving change for justice and avoiding the violence of war.[10]

Palestinian Muslim scholar Mohammed Abu-Nimer describes nonviolent resistance action as effective; it works. It overcomes injustice; it topples dictators, without the massive killing of war. The people of Iran toppled their dictator, the Shah, nonviolently, by massing millions in the streets. Abdul Ghaffar Khan shared with Gandhi in using nonviolent direct action to achieve the independence of India from British colonialism. The first Palestinian Intifada, which was mostly nonviolent action, achieved significant results. It moved Palestine and Israel toward entering into negotiations for the first time, and eventually to the Oslo Accords. But when Israeli leader Benjamin Netanyahu first delayed and then refused to implement the Oslo Accords, Palestinian groups not in agreement with non-violent methods shifted to the violent intifada. This led to enormous violence and moved Israel political parties away from peacemaking and instead toward military attacks against Palestinian leaders, refusal to negotiate, and building The Wall.[11]

Similarly, Chaiwat Satha-Anand advocates "nonviolent action as an Islamic mode of struggle."[12] The practice of withdrawing support from the unjust exercise of power "simply embodies the basic Islamic principle that a person should submit only to the Will of God. As a result, a Muslim is not bound to obey anyone whose power has been used unjustly." He quotes the Qur'an (4:77, 4:97, and 10:62) and says: "Complete submission to the Will of Allah means that if Muslims are oppressed and too weak to fight back, they nevertheless must refuse to obey an unjust ruler.... As a technique, nonviolent action is not passive: 'It is not inaction. It is *action* that is nonviolent.'"

1.2 Independent initiatives

The second practice of just peacemaking, the strategy of *independent initiatives*, is less well known. But it is how we got rid of the most destabilizing nuclear weapons of all, the weapons most likely to start a nuclear war, the medium-range nuclear weapons in Europe. And it is how we got rapid action to remove nuclear weapons from surface ships, and to reduce the number of long-range nuclear weapons from 17,000 to about half that number. The strategy works like this:

1. Take an initiative that decreases distrust and threat perception, by decreasing some offensive threat, but not significantly reducing defensive capability. For example, the halt to testing nuclear weapons, and Gorbachev's removing half the Soviet tanks from West of the Ural mountains.

2. Announce the initiative in advance, clearly explaining you are hoping for some reciprocal initiative, and that if it works, you will take more initiatives, because you want to shift from escalation toward de-escalation.

3. You must take the initiative by the date you promised, even if some hostile words or events occur; you need to decrease distrust so the other side can take some initiatives.

4. Make the initiative clearly visible and verifiable by the other side.

5. Take the initiative independent of waiting for the slow process of negotiations.

6. Take initiatives in a series; it will take more than one to overcome deep distrust.

7. If the other side reciprocates, reward them with additional significant initiatives; if they do not, keep the door open by continuing with a series of small initiatives.

The "Roadmap for Peace in the Middle East" illustrates the just peacemaking practice of *independent initiatives*: Palestine named a Prime Minister different from Arafat, and suspended terrorism for three months, and then later for longer periods of time; Israel pulled back temporarily from occupation of northern Gaza and Bethlehem, and released several prisoners. But then Israel assassinated terrorist leaders, Palestine re-initiated terrorism, and Israel re-occupied. The point of the just peacemaking practice of independent initiatives is to decrease distrust and decrease the sense of threat. It requires persistence, graciousness, and refraining from violence. Ehud Barak took a helpful initiative when he removed Israeli troops from occupying Southern Lebanon, and Ariel Sharon later took a helpful initiative when he withdrew Israeli occupation from Gaza. He announced plans to withdraw much of the occupation from the West Bank as well. Then, in a deliberately provocative action, some radical Palestinians kidnapped one Israeli soldier. And in response, Israel violated the third point in the strategy—to continue despite the inevitable provocations by hawks who want to derail the peace process. Prime Minister Olmert ordered devastating attacks on Gaza in response to the kidnapping of one soldier. Then Hezbollah in Lebanon violated the strategy by kidnapping two Israeli soldiers, and Olmert foolishly ordered devastating destruction against Lebanon. His rating in the polls dropped to about 15%, and he seemed too weak to withdraw occupation from the West Bank. Peace in the Middle East requires firm international support for nonviolent initiatives and against violent retaliatory actions, and for the two-state solution that was the conflict resolution agreement in the Geneva Accords.

1.3 Cooperative conflict resolution

In Matthew 5:21-26, Jesus teaches that if we are angry with someone, we should go talk and make peace. This is the way of grace that God has taken toward us in Christ. God was angry with us for our disobedience and enmity, so God took a grace-based transforming initiative and came to us in Christ and made peace. This is an imperative, a command. It is not, "if you think the one you are angry at is good enough, deserving enough, open-minded enough, then do this"; it is a command from Jesus.

During the days of the Cold War, the Soviet Union and the United States threatened each other enormously, but they had the wisdom to talk with each other and work out numerous treaties and agreements to prevent war.

Likewise, former president Jimmy Carter practiced cooperative conflict resolution in 1994 with North Korea. North Korea agreed to shut down their nuclear reactor and admit continuous UN International Atomic Energy Agency inspections in exchange for the offer of oil to make electricity. Talking worked.

President Carter also worked hard to get prime ministers Anwar Sadat of Egypt and Menachem Begin of Israel to practice cooperative conflict resolution at Camp David. Prior to this, they had refused negotiations. But it worked. Now Israel and Egypt do not threaten each other, and they have peace, even though not an enthusiastic peace. Jordan has followed suit. By contrast, at the present time Israel refuses to talk with Palestine, and they are not making peace.

George W. Bush contradicted the policies of previous administrations that had talked with the Soviet Union, with North Korea, and with other nations where there were hostilities. He treated negotiation as a "reward." He has refused to negotiate with North Korea, Iran, Syria, and Palestine. This is the opposite of Jesus' command to go talk and make peace where there is enmity. And of course it has not worked well. North Korea has been building nuclear weapons, as perhaps has Iran. In June, 2002, the CIA reported that North Korea had gotten twenty centrifuges for enriching uranium from Pakistan. How to respond? James A. Kelly, Assistant Secretary of State, went to talk with North Korea in October. But he was told not to negotiate; he could only give an ultimatum. The North Korean negotiator responded by insisting upon his nation's right to develop nuclear weapons, without saying whether it actually had any. He accused the United States of threatening North Korea's survival, and produced a list of alleged U.S. failures to meet its own obligations under Carter's 1994 agreement. Then he offered to shut down their enrichment program in return for an American promise not to attack and a commitment to normalize relations. Constrained by his instructions, Kelly could only re-state his ultimatum: North Korea must act first. Then the United States halted the oil shipments that had been previously agreed upon.

Without oil, North Korea needed electricity from some source, so they started up their nuclear reactors once again. They said that if the U.S. would sign a treaty of non-aggression, and restore the oil, they would halt their nuclear generators and allow inspections once again. But the U.S. refused negotiations, and North Korea has been running its reactors and producing plutonium for these five years since. Not talking did not work.

Finally, early in 2007, U.S. ambassador Christopher Hill engaged in direct talks with North Korea and restored the 1994 agreement: halt the nuclear generators, receive oil as a substitute, readmit the UN International Atomic Energy Agency with continuous inspections to verify compliance with the agreement, lift the freeze on North Korean money in foreign banks, and look forward to the possibility of peaceful relations between North Korea and the United States. It was five years and fuel for several nuclear bombs late, but finally they talked, and finally they made peace. This is the practice of "cooperative conflict resolution." The alternative would have been more nuclear weapons in North Korea, and the likely acquisition of nuclear weapons by South Korea, Japan, and perhaps other neighbors. This situation has provided an example to Iran to "go and do likewise".

Cooperative conflict resolution, nonviolent direct action, and independent initiatives, all implement the strategy of transforming initiatives:

1. They affirm that the enemy is a member of God's community, loved by God, with some valid interests, even while confronting their unjust actions.

2. They are proactive initiatives of grace and peacemaking, not simply passive resignation.

3. They confront the other with an invitation to make peace that includes justice.

4. They are historically embodied practices, not merely ideals.

5. They acknowledge the log in our own eyes and take responsibility for peacemaking rather than simply judging the other.

1.4 Acknowledge responsibility for conflict and injustice, and seek repentance and forgiveness.

This practice clearly was taught by Jesus. Donald Shriver has argued eloquently in his An Ethic for Enemies that forgiveness in Jesus' teachings is not only an individual matter but a social practice for society as well.[13]

Shriver points to five regular practices that Jesus taught and modeled, all of which built forgiveness into the practice of the community: healings that bought outcasts into community membership; eating with outcasts that similarly brought outcasts into community; the Lord's Prayer that not only emphasized forgiveness but said our being forgiven depends on our forgiving those who have offended us; the community practice of forgiving enemies like Zacchaeus and other tax collectors, Roman soldiers, and those who executed him; and the practice of restorative justice that he taught.

For centuries, realists said we could not expect rulers of nations to repent or give forgiveness; they would lose face, and it would weaken them in their competition for power and interest. So wars are fought over unconfessed injustices that still fester from as long ago as 1389. But a new practice has arisen. German theological ethicist Dietrich Bonhoeffer wrote a confession of his and Germany's guilt during the Nazi period. Then churches in Germany started making confession on Germany's behalf. Christian war resisters from Germany have volunteered their alternative service in other nations that Germany had fought, as an action of reconciliation; three of them have lived in our home during their times of service. Then Willy Brandt, Germany's Chancellor, presented a wreath at the Warsaw Ghetto in Poland in memory of Jews and Poles slaughtered by Germans there. He sank onto his knees in tearful prayer. He announced that Germany would accept the shrunken border of Germany at the Oder Neisse River, and never try to get territory back from Poland. German President Richard von Weizsäcker delivered an eloquent address in the German parliament naming German sins during the Nazi period, and expressing German repentance. The outcome has been repentance and forgiveness between Germany and many of its former enemies, and a present-day Germany transformed into an influence for peacemaking.

The Prime Minister of Japan has finally apologized concretely and in writing to Korea for Japan's atrocities against Koreans, and Korean President Kim Dae Jung responded that this is what Korea has been waiting for, and now cultural and social exchanges may finally take place. Since then, Japanese leaders have backed off some, and it's an ongoing discussion.

President Bush senior finally led Congress to pay reparations to American citizens of Japanese descent unjustly imprisoned and deprived of their property and homes during World War II. President Clinton traveled to Guatemala, and to Africa, to declare repentance on behalf of the United States, and expressed repentance toward African Americans.

Acknowledgment is a new practice of peacemaking that can lance festering boils that threaten to erupt into violence and war. Shriver describes it eloquently. So does the brilliant Croatian-American theologian, Miroslav Volf, a Fuller graduate, in his moving book, *Exclusion and Embrace*.[14] The practice of repentance and forgiveness, so clearly taught and practiced by Jesus, is now spreading among nations and is acting to abolish emotions that cause wars.

2. Justice: human rights and sustainable economic development

Jesus cared deeply about justice, as God does. We can see this in myriad ways.

New Testament scholars are paying new attention to Jesus' attack on the Temple system as a major clue to why he was crucified, and to his understanding of his mission. This was neither an act of violent revolution, nor merely a "cleansing" of the temple, but a symbolic prophetic action of protest against injustice and its cover-up.[15] "Jesus does not seek to purify current temple worship but symbolically attacks the very function of the temple and heralds its destruction." His hostility to the temple emerges as a charge at his trial and as a taunt at the cross (Mark 14:58 and 15:29). N.T. Wright points out that in six different passages, Jesus prophesied the destruction of the Temple: Mark 13; 14:58; 15:29-30; John 2:9; Acts 6:14: Thomas 71.[16]

Jesus cited two prophetic passages as he carried out this prophetic action. Isaiah 56:7, "My house shall be called a house of prayer for all the nations," is part of the declaration in Isaiah 56:1-8 that God's purpose is to bless all who are being excluded, the foreigners, eunuchs, and outcasts. Repeatedly during his ministry, Jesus confronted the authorities for the injustice of their exclusion of outcasts, handicapped, and Gentiles. The temple had become a nationalistic symbol of this unjust exclusion, which was in direct contradiction to the prophecies of Isaiah.

Jeremiah 7 says we should not keep claiming we have the Temple of the Lord, when we need to amend our ways and truly execute justice, not oppress the alien, the orphan, or the widow, or shed innocent blood and go after other gods. If we continue to practice injustice, God will destroy the Temple and cast us out of God's sight. By quoting from Jeremiah 7, Jesus attacks "a false trust in the efficacy of the temple sacrificial system. The leaders of the people think that they can rob widows' houses (Mark 12:40) and then perform the prescribed sacrifices according to the prescribed patterns at the prescribed times in the prescribed purity in the prescribed sacred space and then be safe and secure from all alarms."[17]

N.T. Wright begins *Jesus and the Victory of God* with the thesis that has emerged out of his massive study: "I shall argue, first, that Jesus' public persona within first-century Judaism was that of a prophet, and [second] that the content of his prophetic proclamation was the 'kingdom' of Israel's God."[18] "The prophetic aspect of Jesus' work is often surprisingly ignored," but Wright gives a synopsis of the verses seeing him as a prophet mighty in word and deed.[19] The prophets of Israel again and again announced that God wills justice to the powerless - the orphans, widows, poor, and immigrants. The four Hebrew and Greek words for justice occur 1,060 times in the Bible. Hardly any other word is repeated so often. If we do not read Hebrew and Greek, we may not recognize this, because the two Hebrew words are often translated as righteousness and judgment, but they mean the kind of justice that delivers the powerless from their oppression and bondage into covenant community.[20]

The kingdom of God has suffered misunderstanding as well. N.T. Wright writes that the kingdom of God was well understood in Jesus' Jewish context: It meant the reign of God as the prophets prophesied: not the end of the space-time universe, not the "cosmic meltdown." The crucial question is "not so much the kingdom's *timing* as its *content*."[21] Jesus clearly affirmed and enacted four marks of the kingdom of God that we see in the prophets: God will be present like the light of day; God will save us, deliver us, forgive us; God will bring peace; and God will bring justice. Just look at passages like Isaiah 9:6-7; 52:7; Isaiah 60 and 61, and Psalm 37: again and again you will see the four marks: God's presence, salvation, justice and peace. And also joy, healing, and return to God.

I count 40 times in the Synoptic Gospels, not including parallels, when Jesus confronts the hierarchy or the wealthy for injustice, such as seeking prestige and wealth and not lifting a finger to lift the burdens of the poor and oppressed. By "the hierarchy," I mean the Sadducees and the representatives of the Temple hierarchy, including Pharisees, who were the day-to-day authorities that Jews encountered, plus the Herods and Pilates and Roman rulers.

The prophets say again and again that injustice causes the destruction of war, and that when we repent and practice justice, then peace will follow. Jesus fulfills this prophetic witness to God's compassion for justice. Therefore, just peacemaking theory has two practices of justice.

2.1 Democracy, human rights, and religious liberty.

When Jimmy Carter, a faithful Baptist who was determined to express his faith in a way that could also be translated into public language, became president of the U. S., he had already stood courageously for human rights in Georgia's struggle to overcome racial discrimination and segregation. He announced that U.S. foreign policy would examine the human rights record of other countries, and U.S. foreign aid would be contingent on it. Furthermore, the Roman Catholic church committed itself to work for human rights especially when Pope John XXIII was Pope, and when the Second Vatican Council did its work in 1963. Other denominations also pushed for human rights around the world. Partly as a result, Latin America, which used to be mostly military dictatorships, is now all democracies with attention to human rights or at least is officially moving in that direction despite the power of elites and militaries. Democracy is spreading in many previous dictatorships in Central and Eastern Europe, and in South Korea, Taiwan, and Indonesia, and others, as has long been true of India. When we participate in churches that encourage this spread, and join human rights groups, we strengthen this trend. And here is the peacemaking payoff: not one democracy with human rights has fought a war against another democracy with human rights in the whole twentieth century. The data sources from the discipline of international relations are there in the book, *Just Peacemaking.*

Just Peacemaking also clearly states that democracy should be spread by pushing for human rights and religious liberty, and not by wars of intervention. "External military intervention, even against the most odious dictators, is a dangerous way to produce a democratic world order. . . . Any time an outside power supplants any existing government, the problem of legitimacy is paramount. The very democratic norms to be instilled may be compromised."[22] The resulting culture tends to be more violent, with opponents to the new government saying "this government was imposed by foreign intervention and patriots will fight against it," while the victors foster a culture that says "our freedom depends on making war"—as has often been said by U.S. defenders of the Iraq War.

2.2 *Just and sustainable economic development*

that focuses on building communities is crucial for peacemaking. I think of Carl Ryther, Baptist agricultural missionary, whose methods were crucial in transforming Bangladesh into self-sustaining in the area of food. I think of Mushéshé and the Uganda Rural Development Project, which he has led and which I have visited, transforming the lives of rural Ugandans in the western part of the country. I think of Bread for the World, and of Ron Sider's book, *Rich Christians in an Age of Hunger*.

Terrorism and violent rebellion tend to come from people who experience a worsening of economic or human rights conditions by comparison with what they had expected. In political science literature, this is called "relative deprivation"—relative to their expectations. Not the absolute poor, but those who had good reason to expect things to be better than present worse conditions. So peacemaking requires sustainable development—the kind that is steady and not deeply disappointing, and that spreads empowerment widely, rather than concentrating it in the hands of the wealthy while others are driven into despair.

3. Strengthening cooperative forces

The third group of peacemaking practices may be seen as a dimension of love understood realistically, rather than sentimentally: a key dimension of love in scriptural teaching is breaking down barriers to community. When Jesus taught "Love your enemies," he was saying God gives rain and sunshine to the just and the unjust alike. Therefore, we must include even our enemies in the community of neighbors (Matthew 5:44-45). Jesus was interpreting Leviticus 19:17-18—we are to love our neighbors as ourselves—and teaching that we are to include all persons to whom God gives sunshine and rain in the community of neighbors. Similarly the prophet Isaiah says we are to be a light to the nations.

How can we implement this love and light in the world of nations? Surely it means that we must include the nations of the world in networks of relationships—treaties, trade, communication, immigration, international study, dialogue and discussion.

Furthermore, a realistic understanding of human nature teaches us that all persons, and all nations and all political leaders, have a proclivity to sin. The apostle Paul writes, "all have sinned and fallen short of the glory of God" (Romans 3:23). Therefore realism argues that all nations need the check and balance of the wisdom of other nations, giving them correction when they are tempted to do wrong. To think that "our" government is the exception, and does not sin, and therefore does not need the checks and balances of international cooperation, is, Christianly speaking, heresy. It also keeps us from learning from our errors and making the right corrections the next time, and so is, realistically speaking, foolishness.

3.1 Recognize emerging cooperative forces in the international system, and work with them

Generations of leaders have worked to develop international networks of treaties, nongovernmental organizations, international cooperation, international travel and communication, international study, economic trade relations, emigration and immigration, international church organizations and missions, so that we are knitted together with networks that work to prevent war. Many returned from World War II determined to do what they could to prevent World War III and nuclear war. They built an impressive array of treaties and international networks of cooperation. And the empirical evidence in political science is clear: nations that are more engaged in international networks of cooperation make war less often.

3.2 Strengthen the United Nations and international efforts for cooperation and human rights

States float in a sea of forces from outside their borders. Acting alone, they cannot solve problems of trade, debt, interest rates; of pollution, ozone depletion, acid rain, depletion of fish stocks, global warming; of migrations and refugees seeking asylum; of military security when weapons rapidly penetrate borders.

Therefore, cooperative action is increasingly necessary. We should press governments to act in small and large crises in ways that strengthen the effectiveness of the United Nations, of regional organizations, and of multilateral peacemaking, peacekeeping, and peace building. Many multilateral practices are building effectiveness to resolve conflicts, to monitor, nurture, and even enforce truces and replace violent conflict with beginning cooperation. They are organizing to meet human needs for food, hygiene, medicine, education, and economic interaction. Furthermore, most wars now happen within states, not between states. Therefore, *Just Peacemaking* contends that collective action needs to include UN-approved humanitarian intervention in cases like the former Yugoslavia, Haiti, Somalia, and Rwanda "when a state's condition or behavior results in . . . grave and massive violations of human rights."

The United Nations is not perfect, but the world needs checks and balances against rash responses and unwise actions by all nations. We do not want a world of anarchy, but a world that has some laws, some checks and balances. Empirical data show that nations that cooperate more actively with various United Nations and regional organizations make war less frequently.

3.3 Reduce offensive weapons and weapons trade

Jesus teaches, "Put up your sword. Those who take up the sword, by the sword will die" (Matthew 26:52). In Jesus' context, there was great resentment against Roman occupation of Israel's homeland. Now and then a guerrilla leader would claim to be a Messiah and lead a revolt against Rome. Jesus taught against taking up weapons; it would lead to the destruction of the temple and of Jerusalem. He wept over Jerusalem because "you do not know the practices of peace." He taught constructive peacemaking initiatives to oppose and correct the injustice by *nonviolent* means, from which we are drawing the practices of just peacemaking theory. His prophecy was validated when the resentment against Roman occupation boiled over into a major rebellion against Rome in C.E. 66. Rome retaliated, destroyed the temple, destroyed Jerusalem, and exiled Jews from their homeland.

This is the context for the teachings of Jesus about constructive initiatives of peacemaking. His teachings of peacemaking practices are not merely scattered prooftexts; they are a consistent strategy supported by wisdom in the context of occupation. In our time, with almost infinitely more destructive weapons, the context cries out for all of us to teach constructive practices of peacemaking. This is realism in the face of such destructive power.

But there is another context as well: the will of God for peace. God's will is not merely a distant ideal. It is specific and concrete. And one specific teaching is that reliance on military weapons while disdaining the practices of peace is idolatry and leads to destruction (Isaiah 30, 31; Jeremiah 2).

A key factor in the decrease of war between nations is the reality that weapons have become so destructive that war is not worth the price. The offense cannot destroy the defense before it does huge retaliatory damage. Reducing offensive weapons and shifting toward defensive force structures strengthens that equation. For example, Gorbachev removed half the Soviet Union's tanks from Central Europe and all its river-crossing equipment. This freed NATO to agree to get rid of all medium-range and shorter-range nuclear weapons on both sides from Eastern and Western Europe— the first dramatic step in ending the Cold War peacefully.

The war in Bosnia is the counterexample that proves the rule: Serbia controlled the former Yugoslavian army and its weapons, so their offensive weapons tempted them to make war, thinking there wouldn't be much retaliation. Milosevic made three wars—against Bosnia-Herzegovina, against Croatia, and against Kosovo. The results were disastrous. Likewise, the U.S. military budget is greater than all other nations combined. It, too, faces the temptation to make wars, thinking there won't be disastrous consequences.

As nations turn toward democracy and human rights, their governments no longer need large militaries to keep them in power. Arms imports by developing nations in 1995 dropped to one-quarter of their peak in 1988. Not all nations are following suit, however. In some cases, the political power of weapons manufacturers is inordinately strong.

3.4 Encourage grassroots peacemaking
groups and voluntary associations

Like the prophets of Israel, Jesus gathered a group of disciples to learn the practices and carry on the mission. He would die; they would need to carry on the message. He traveled from village to village, organizing cell groups of followers to spread his teachings.

Accordingly just peacemaking requires cell groups of believers organized independently of governments and linked together across boundaries of nation, class, and race, to learn peacemaking practices and press governments to employ these practices.

The existence of a growing worldwide people's movement constitutes a force that can partially transcend captivity by narrow national or ideological perspectives. Citizens' groups are not so committed to status-quo institutional maintenance as bureaucracies often are, nor are they as isolated and only temporarily engaged as lone individuals often are, and so they can provide long-term perseverance in peacemaking. Churches and church groups can serve as voices for the voiceless, as they did in churches in East Germany and in women's groups in Guatemala.[23] They can help to initiate, foster, or support transforming initiatives, where existing parties need support and courage to take risks to break out of the cycles that perpetuate violence and injustice. A citizens' network of NGO's and INGO's can often be a source of information and knowledge that persons in positions of governmental authority lack or resist. They can criticize injustice and initiate repentance and forgiveness. They can nurture a spirituality that sustains courage when just peacemaking is unpopular, hope when despair or cynicism is tempting, and grace and forgiveness when just peacemaking fails. The challenge is to encourage Christians and other citizens to gather together in churches and other peacemaking groups, to do the practices of peacemaking, and to prod governments to engage in the practices of peacemaking.

4. But it won't be easy

There are powerful economic interests and natural drives for national security that work for good or evil. There are interests that do not want to make peace, and interests that think the way to peace is to threaten or destroy the enemy. There are enormous forces of evil: nuclear weapons and their delivery systems; chemical and biological weapons; devastating poverty and its offspring of population explosion; ecological devastation and nonrenewable energy consumption; ethnic and religious wars within nations like Congo, Somalia, Iraq, Afghanistan, and Palestine-Israel. "Some 2 million children have died in dozens of wars during the past decade. . . . Today, civilians account for more than 90 percent of war casualties."[24] Each peacemaking practice recognizes and seeks to resolve, lessen, discipline, or check and balance one or more of these negative forces.

Endnotes

1 Glen Stassen, ed., *Just Peacemaking: Ten Practices for Abolishing War* (Pilgrim: 1998; 2004). This essay will refer to the ten practices of just peacemaking as set forth in this book.

2 Glen Stassen, *Just Peacemaking: Transforming Initiatives for Justice and Peace* (Westminster John Knox: 1992).

3 See the old, but excellent, book by Norman Gottwald in his less controversial period, *All The Kingdoms of the Earth: Israelite Prophecy and International Relations in the Ancient Near East* (Harper & Row: 1964), on the peacemaking practices proclaimed by the prophets of Israel.

4 Walter Wink, "Neither Passivity Nor Violence: Jesus' Third Way," in *The Love of Enemy and Nonretaliation in the New Testament*, ed.

Willard Swartley (Westminster/John Knox: 1992), 114f. N. T. Wright, *Jesus and the Victory of God* (Fortress Press: 1996), 290-1.

5   Clarence Jordan, *The Substance of Faith and Other Cotton Patch Sermons*, ed. Dallas Lee (New York: Association Press, 1972), 69.

6   Try it: lift your right hand; imagining you are slapping someone on the *right* cheek. You will be giving a back-handed slap.

7   See Stassen, *Just Peacemaking: Transforming Initiatives*, chapter 3, for a fuller explanation. Also Stassen, *Living the Sermon on the Mount: A Practical Hope for Grace and Deliverance* (San Francisco: Jossey Bass, 2006), and "The Fourteen Triads of the Sermon on the Mount: Matthew 5:21-7:12," *Journal of Biblical Literature* 122/2 (Summer, 2003), 267-308.

8   (Grand Rapids: Eerdmans: 1972; 1993), chapter 5.

9   John Domenic Crossan, *The Historical Jesus* (New York: Harper San Francisco, 1991), 135f.

10   Daniel Buttry, *Christian Peacemaking: From Heritage to Hope* (Valley Forge: Judson, 1994).

11   *Nonviolence and Peacebuilding in Islam*, 14-15, 36, and 87.

12   Chaiwat Satha-anand (Qader Muheideen), in *Peace and Conflict Resolution in Islam*, 204-209.

13   Donald Shriver, *An Ethic for Enemies: Forgiveness in Politics* (Oxford: 1995), 36.

14   *Exclusion and Embrace: A Theological Exploration of Identity, Otherness, and Reconciliation* (Abingdon: 1996).

15   David Garland, *Mark: The NIV Application Commentary* (Zondervan: 1996), 433-9.

16   Wright, *Jesus and the Victory of God*, 335.

17   Garland.

18   Wright 11. Representative pages showing the biblical witness to Jesus' acting in the tradition of the prophets are 93, 97, and 116, but the evidence is amassed throughout the book. He discusses Jesus' announcement of the kingdom of God on 20f., 40, 50, 72, 101f.

19   Wright, 164f.

20   See Stassen, *Just Peacemaking: Transforming Initiatives for Justice and Peace*, 71ff.

21   Wright, 221.

22 Ibid., 114.

23 Jörg Swoboda, *Revolution of the Candles* (Atlanta, GA: Mercer University, 1997); and Michelle Tooley, *Voices of the Voiceless* (Scottdale, PA: Herald, 1997).

24 Desmond Tutu, "Stop Killing the Children," *The Washington Post,* November 24, 1996, C7.

About the Contributors
to this Book

Azar Ajaj is a graduate of Bethlehem Bible College. He has served in Israel as the General Secretary of the International Fellowship of Evangelical Students. He is currently working with the Bible Society in Israel as the director of the ministry among the Israeli Arabs. He is also teaching at the Nazareth Extension of Bethlehem Bible College, and is a graduate student in the M.Th. programme in Biblical Studies at the International Baptist Theological Seminary in Prague, Czech Republic.

Mubarak Awad is a Palestinian-American psychologist and advocate of nonviolent resistance. Awad, a Christian, was born in 1943 in Jerusalem during the British Mandate. Mubarak's father was killed in 1948 during the fighting between Jews and Arabs. As his house was left in disputed "no man's land," he became a refugee in the old city of Jerusalem. After higher education in USA, Mr. Awad was given the right to Israeli citizenship in 1967, but refused and kept his Palestinian and USA citizenship. In 1985, Awad established the Palestinian Centre for the Study of Nonviolence, prior to the first *intifada*, In the Middle East he is called the Arab Gandhi because he was teaching the power of nonviolence similar to Mahatma Gandhi. Israel deported Awad in 1988. He returned to the United States, where he founded the organization *Nonviolence International*, working in more than six countries to promote nonviolent resistance and human rights. Mubarak Awad is married to Nancy Nye and has two children, Tamara and Karim, who are living and working in Canada.

Wesley H. Brown is the former chaplain and an adjunct tutor in Contexual Missiology at the International Baptist Theological Seminary in Prague. He and his wife, Dr. Cheryl A. Brown, served 7 years in theological education with the European Baptist Federation. Previously he was President of the American Baptist Seminary of the West in Berkeley, California, USA, and earlier was Middle East representative in Jerusalem for the American Baptist Churches. He also served for 13 years in Congo in theological education. He earned his Ph.D. at the University of Southern California in USA. He now lives in Claremont, California, USA in Pilgrim Place, a retirement community for Christian pastors, missionaries, and theological educators.

Ronald E. Diprose (Ph.D. hons) completed his undergraduate study in Theology with the University of Melbourne (Australia). Later he gained an M.A. (hons) in New Testament studies at Trinity Evangelical Divinity School (Deerfield, Illinois, USA). In his doctoral dissertation, presented to the faculty of the *Evangelische Theologische Faculteit* (Leuven, Belgium) in 1997, he examined the way Israel features in the development of Christian thought, as documented in early Christian writings, and following the Shoah. Part of this work has since been published in Italian, German, French and English (*Israel and the Church*). He is Academic Dean at the *Instituto Biblico Evangelico Italiano* (Rome), is a lecturer at the Nazareth Centre of Christian Studies and Editor of the theological journal *Lux Biblica*.

David Friedman is a professor of Jewish studies who taught for 23 years in post-secondary education in Israel. He is also a Messianic rabbi who has served as a synagogue rabbi. He was born in Germany, son of a human rights attorney. He earned a B.A. in Theology at Valparaiso University, a Master's degree in Arabic at the University of Minnesota, and a Ph.D. in Jewish Studies at California Graduate School of Theology. He is the author of four books, the latest is *Sudden Terror*, and has been involved in reconciliation efforts in Israel, Holland, and the USA.

Wilrens L. Hornstra (1961) is a citizen of the Netherlands and lives in Germany, where he is a lecturer at Youth With A Mission's School in Biblical Studies. From 2002 to 2007 he wrote his doctoral dissertation at the Oxford Centre for Mission Studies on Christian Zionism among Evangelicals in post-war Germany.

Yohanna Katanacho is a Palestinian Evangelical. He has earned his M.A. from Wheaton College and his Ph.D. from Trinity Evangelical Divinity School. Katanacho has written two Arabic books, many articles, and has translated three books from English to Arabic. He is now serving as the director of the academic affairs at Bethlehem Bible College—Galilee Extension. Katanacho has spoken in many churches and conferences unpacking theological perspectives on the Arab-Israeli conflict.

Lisa Loden has lived in Israel since 1974. She is a co-founder of Messianic congregation Beit Asaph in Netanya, Israel. From 2002-2007 she served as the Director of the Caspari Center for Biblical and Jewish Studies in Jerusalem, writes for *Mishkan* – a Journal of the Gospel and the Jewish People, served as a member of the International Board of Lausanne Consultation on Jewish Evangelism from 1999-2007, is chairman of the local board of *Christian Witness to Israel*, serves on *Musalaha Reconciliation Ministries* advisory board and chairs the women's work for Musalaha. She is currently on the faculty of the Nazareth Center for Christian Studies and heads up their Leadership Development Program.

Peter F. Penner was born in Kazakhstan (1961) and is a citizen of Germany. He has been in leadership with St. Petersburg Christian University (Russia) for 10 years and is presently at the International Baptist Theological Seminary (6 years) serving in Mission and Biblical Studies. He received his Master's degree in the US (Mennonite Brethren Biblical Seminary, Fresno) and his Th.D. in South Africa (UNISA). In the last 20 years he has been involved in different capacities, publishing different articles and IBTS conference documents.

Philip Saa'd is the Pastor of the Arab Baptist Church in Haifa, Israel. He is a graduate of the Hebrew University of Jerusalem, and an M.Div. graduate of Mid America Baptist Theological Seminary, Memphis, TN, USA. He is known in Israel for his warm relationship with Messianic believers in Jesus in Israel as well as for being a strong Arab Baptist leader.

Glen H. Stassen is the author of *Living the Sermon on the Mount* (Jossey Bass: July, 2006), *Kingdom Ethics: Following Jesus in Contemporary Context*, with David Gushee (InterVarsity, 2003), and *Just Peacemaking: Transforming Initiatives for Justice and Peace* (Westminster/John Knox: 1992). *Kingdom Ethics* won the *Christianity Today* Award for Best Book of 2004 in Theology or Ethics. He is Lewis B. Smedes Professor of Christian Ethics at Fuller Theological Seminary in Pasadena, California, USA, where he won the All Seminary Council Faculty Award for Outstanding Community Service to Students.

Index

A

B

C

as *hudna, 79*
Oslo Interim Agreements, 26
Ottoman Empire, 15
Ouwneel, Willem, 70-71

P

Palestine Liberation Organization (PLO), 23
Palestinian Arabs, orientation of, 150
Palestinian Authority (PA), establishment of, 25-26
Palestinian Christians, 150-151
    Christian Zionists and, 64
    difficulty attending reconciliation meetings and, 153-154
    diversity of, 151
    endangerment of, 117
    gospel proclamation by, 108
    "the great catastrophe" and, 17, 56
    liberation theology, 10
    Messianic Jews and, 109
    Muslim discrimination and, 79
    number of, 162
    Old Testament and, 114-115
    perspectives of, 112
    rejection of dispensationalism by, 114
    view of a Palestinian State, 27
    West Bank/Gaza settlements and, 23, 26
    women
        reconciliation activities of, 149–159
    see also Arab Christians
Palestinian church
    liberation theology and, 151
    supersessionism and, 151
Palestinian Islamic Resistance Movement, claim to ownership of
  Palestine by, 109
Palestinian Liberation Organization (PLO), 23, 69
Palestinian State, views on, 27-28
Palestinian theology of the Land, 113–114
Palestinians
    Christian Zionists and, 64
    as part of Gog and Magog, 52-53
    suffering of, Christians ignoring, 24-25
    view of a Palestinian State, 27
Parsons, David, 25
Paul, on national election, 99

THE INTERNATIONAL BAPTIST THEOLOGICAL SEMINARY OF THE EUROPEAN BAPTIST FEDERATION O.P.S.

The Revd Dr. Keith G. Jones MA, Rector

The International Baptist Theological Seminary (IBTS) is situated on the beautiful European Baptist Centre campus in the historic Šárka Valley in Prague 6, just a few minutes away from the Prague castle area. It is wholly owned by the European Baptist Federation (EBF), which comprises fifty two Baptist Unions in membership throughout Europe, the Middle East and Central Asia.

IBTS was founded in 1952 in Switzerland initially to train pastors for service in central and southern Europe. IBTS moved to Prague following the collapse of communism and our newly renovated premises were opened in 1997.

IBTS has expanded its mission and ministry since the first years in Switzerland and now offers an exciting range of academic, research and conference activities as follows –

Higher research degrees
Doctor of Philosophy and Master of Philosophy
(Validated by the University of Wales, Great Britain)

Post Graduate degrees
Magister in Theology (A second cycle European Union "Bologna" degree accredited by the Czech Republic Ministry of Education)

Master of Theology in either Applied Theology, Baptist/Anabaptist Studies, Biblical Studies or Contextual Missiology (validated by the University of Wales)

Research Institutes
Baptist and Anabaptist Studies. Founded 1982. Sponsors of the Hughey Lectureship

Mission and Evangelism. Founded 1988.

Biblical Studies. Founded 2004.

Systematic Studies of Contextual Theologies. Founded 2004. Sponsors of the Nordenhaug Lectures

Specialist Theological Library
Over 69,000 volume specialist theology library, principally in the English language.

Conferences and Courses
Each year a range of relevant international conferences organised by IBTS and our Research Institutes on contemporary issues of mission and theology.

IBTS
Nad Habrovkou 3, 164 00 Praha 6, Czech Republic
www.ibts.eu

Made in the USA